The Blue-Collar Prophet: How & Why God Wants to Speak Through You!

THE BLUE-COLLAR PROPHET

Published by
Dwight A. Clough dba Creative Advantage
311 West Main Street, Sun Prairie, WI 53590-2909

ISBN: 0-9670718-2-8

Most scripture quotations are taken from the Holy Bible,
New International Version, copyright © 1973, 1978, 1984
by the International Bible Society.

Printed in the USA

To my family,
With deepest gratitude.
Tom Stamman

Special thanks to:

- **Steven Kozar** whose painting is featured on the front cover. To learn more about Steven Kozar and his work visit www.stevenkozar.com.

- **Laura Smith** and **Jeanette Clough** for proofreading.

- **Jeff Highman** for his work with cover design.

- **Mark McConley** of Printing Plus for his gracious assistance with printing.

TABLE OF CONTENTS

Foreword by Warren Heckman

The prophetic ministry has come into prominence in recent years. Many people advertise themselves as prophets and prophetesses. Magazines like *Charisma* display many advertisements for prophetic ministries and meetings. This is a ministry that is often controversial and many times severely criticized. There have been many "wanna-be" prophets who have caused considerable confusion and created chaos for pastors. Consequently, many have avoided the prophetic ministry to avoid the possible problems. But we need all of God's gifts to function within our local churches.

Tom Stamman has ministered for us in Lake City Church, Madison, Wisconsin numerous times over the past years. First, he came to conduct Evangelism Seminars. But, in recent years, his ministry has been to preach, pray for people, and then often to pray prophetically over them. He has always asked us (the Pastoral staff) to stand with him, listen, evaluate and even correct if necessary. He has brought forth words from the Lord that have set people free (deliverance), and brought clarity (wisdom), repentance, reconciliation, healing and hope. People have wept, rejoiced, worshipped, cried out to God, turned their lives over to the Lord, and simply been renewed.

Yes, prophecy and the prophetic are often controversial. This book may be controversial to you as you read it. But, hopefully, it will stir you up to re-examine the Scriptures and "covet earnestly the gift of prophecy" for your life and ministry. So, even if you do not agree with everything that Tom Stamman writes, read it and be encouraged to seek God.

Pastor Warren Heckman
Lake City Church
Madison, Wisconsin
May 15, 2002

A word from Tom Stamman

We are excited that you are taking the time to read this book. We want you to understand God's deep desire to speak to His people through the timeless ministry known in the Scriptures as the prophetic. Whether you've had any personal experience with the prophetic, or not, this book will ...

☐ explain how God speaks to people today.
☐ answer your questions about the prophetic.
☐ examine what the Bible has to say about the prophetic.
☐ inspire you to "covet earnestly the best gifts," and learn how God can use you in this powerful and wonderful ministry.

I challenge you to read this book, and let the Holy Spirit inspire you to become all you can be. May you come to an understanding of how much God loves people and how deeply He desires to speak to His creation.

In this book, I've shared many stories from my own experience. Please understand that the purpose is not to exalt myself. My only purpose is to show how, in similar situations, God can use you. My hope and dream is that you also will be able to share your own personal testimonies of what God has done in your life.

Tom Stamman
Impact Ministries International

CHAPTER 1:
God wants to speak through you.

"Are you jealous for my sake? I wish that all the Lord's people were prophets and that the Lord would put his Spirit on them!"[1] -- Moses, the man of God

In the middle of a gang fight

I didn't expect to find myself in the middle of a gang fight in Fennimore, Wisconsin. If you can find Fennimore on a map, and that's a big "if," you'll see that's it's far, far away from urban USA.

But small town or not, there they were, dozens of guys, bristling in the parking lot, ready to go at it.

It was late and I was ready to call it a day. I had preached a couple of times, I had prayed for dozens of people inside the church building nearby. I was drained.

But my wife said, "Can you witness to those guys?"

I wanted to say, "No."

But then my son looked at me and said, "Dad, can you do it?"

Of course, I had to be the macho man.

I said, "Okay, I can do it."

---

[1] Numbers 11:29

A minute later, armed with a few tracts, I walked out there.

I didn't realize what I was walking into. My wife had the feeling that some of the guys had guns. She had the feeling that this might get violent. It might get bloody. But, she didn't bother to mention any of this to me. I just walked out there, right into the middle of the crowd.

I started preaching to the whole group. The reception was mixed. One kid kept picking on me like he wanted to fight me. He kept saying, "Come on, let's fight. Come on, let's go."

I didn't pay much attention to him. Instead, I was witnessing to another guy who had just come back from the Mardi Gras at New Orleans. God was moving on his heart.

I moved from him to other kids. I started praying for them and casting devils out of them. It was a powerful move of God right there in the parking lot.

Then this huge guy walked up. This guy had muscles on his eyeballs. He was full of tatoos, and meaner than the junkyard dog. He made LeRoy Brown look like an angel.

He walked up to me and he said, "I hate ..." and he named about five ethnic groups. I wasn't one of them, for which I was grateful. "But," he continued, "worse than that, I hate preachers."

That didn't make me feel very good.

At this point, my wife joined me. She whispered to me, "Ask him why he's mad at God."

I said, "Why are you mad at God?"

He didn't answer.

I said, "Because your dad abused you, isn't it?"

He said, "Huh!" and he walked away.

I said, "It's because your dad abused you, isn't it?"

"Huh!" he said.

Finally, he said, "Yeah."

His hard shell was broken, and I ministered to him. I got a chance to pray for him. Here he was -- wanting to beat me up -- and a couple minutes later I was praying for him.

Before I left, the young man who got saved told me, "There were guns here tonight. Young people from two towns were getting together to fight."

But Jesus showed up.

There were guns present. Anything could have happened. My family and I could have been in great danger. But, instead, God used us to turn this gang fight into an opportunity for the gospel. The devil had a plan for that evening, but God turned that plan for evil into an opportunity for good.

How did God do it? He spoke through my wife. And He spoke through me. How did we know what to say?

This book answers that question.

God wants to speak through you. This book will show you how.

What is blue-collar prophecy?

We chose the title, *The Blue-Collar Prophet*, because prophecy is a gift that is available to regular people, ordinary people, just like you and me. Blue-collar prophecy is not just for the spiritually elite or those who are full-time ministers, but for all of those who are believers in the Lord Jesus. The Bible encourages us to desire spiritual gifts, especially the gift of prophecy.[2] It

---

[2]   1 Corinthians 14:1

says, "you can all prophesy ..."[3] The wonderful gift of God speaking through people is available to you, if you are a child of God.

In December of 1999 I had the opportunity to minister in one of the fastest growing churches in Madison, Wisconsin. The pastor, Shane Holden, started the church with a handful of people and within four years they were averaging over 700 people. As we were eating lunch, he shared with me a prophetic word. "You need to write a book on the prophetic," he urged me. Even though there are many wonderful works written by people who have been in the prophetic a lot longer than myself, he explained that the prophetic ministry that I was involved in was unique. Most prophetic ministries minister to leaders of churches, denominations, businesses and governments. Our ministry focuses on the average person and his every day activities. Pastor Shane suggested calling the book *Blue-Collar Prophecy.*

To help you better understand blue-collar prophecy, let's look at it from five perspectives: (1) the person sharing, (2) the type of people receiving the prophetic word, (3) the kind of word they receive, (4) the method used in sharing, and (5) the timing of the prophetic word.

(1) The person sharing.

God has always used blue-collar workers in the prophetic. Amos[4] and Elisha[5] were farmers. Peter was a

---

[3] 1 Corinthians 14:31
[4] Amos 7:14
[5] 1 Kings 19:19

fisherman.[6] David was a shepherd and a king.[7] Joel prophesied that servants and handmaidens would prophesy.[8] In these last days, God will not only use "professional preachers," but laymen like you and me. Blue-collar prophecy occurs when God anoints average Christian believers who love the Lord and inspires them to speak his will and his ways to others.

And the gift of prophesy is not limited to men. God also uses women.[9] Throughout the Word of God we read how God used females in a powerful way. Some of the great prophetic women were Huldah,[10] Hannah,[11] Mary,[12] and Deborah.[13] Women have special needs and interests that only women can truly understand. It's no wonder that God raises up women to move in the prophetic.

The anointing of God is not limited to age. God spoke through Simeon and Anna,[14] both of whom may have been in their eighties. At the other end of the spectrum, God uses children.[15] The Bible says your sons and daughters will prophesy.[16] Jesus said that the greatest in the kingdom of God are little children.[17] God wants to raise up

---

[6] Mark 1:16, Matthew 16:17-18
[7] 2 Samuel 7:8
[8] Joel 2:29
[9] 1 Corinthians 11:5 and many other passages
[10] 2 Chronicles 34:22
[11] 1 Samuel 2:1-10
[12] Luke 1:46-55
[13] Judges 4 & 5
[14] Luke 2:25-38
[15] See Chapter 7 for an inspiring story of God using a two-year old to bring an amazing prophetic word.
[16] Joel 2:28
[17] Matthew 18:4

children to speak His will to His people. Although children have many weaknesses, yet, if they are unhindered by fear, they have a unique way of speaking the truth without glossing it over. In the New Testament we read that Phillip the evangelist had four daughters who prophesied.[18] I would encourage any parent who has a child hungry for God to read this book and let God equip them in the prophetic.

Husband and wife teams can prophesy. Isaiah and his wife apparently both moved in the prophetic.[19] It's a special treat for me when my wife comes along with me and we get to minister together. God often gives her prophecies for people. Even though God primarily uses me, the Lord loves to see his children working together to bring health and well-being to his church.

(2) The type of person receiving:

A number of years ago I was ministering in a rural church in South Dakota. Sitting in the back row was an unassuming man. There was nothing in his outward appearance to make him look flashy or important. But the Lord directed me to call him forward for prayer.

"Sir, in the back row," I said, "I want to pray for you."

He was so shocked that a preacher had called him out to give him a prophetic word that he turned around to see who was behind him -- even though his chair was backed up against the wall! As I ministered to him, I saw God touch him in a way that he had never been touched

---

[18] Acts 21:8-9
[19] Implied in Isaiah 8:3

before. He may have been to prophetic meetings before. But, this time, it was different. This time, God spoke to him.

Many of us have attended conferences or revivals and listened to the prophetic voice of God minister to leaders at a convention. You can just imagine how encouraged these men and women must feel after the prophetic voice of God speaks into their lives. Yet, multitudes sit in the meeting wishing and hoping and praying that God will speak to them. I want to let you know God wants to speak to you.

Blue-collar prophecy is not reserved for the elite, the leading ministers, the heavy hitters in the church, or for the wealthy. Blue-collar prophecy is for each one of us who need a reassuring or confirming word.

Think about it. God is so passionately in love with us that He sacrificed His only Son[20] to bring us into His family. Do you think He wants to wait until we get to heaven before He talks to us? No. He wants to begin the process of intimately knowing Him right now.[21] Personalized prophecy cements our relationship with Jesus, because through prophetic words we know that He knows us. That is why God is raising up prophets in these last days, so every one of us who desire to hear the Father's voice can encounter the heart-pounding experience of God speaking to us.

But the prophetic words are not just reserved for dedicated Christians. Just as God spoke to backsliders and

---

[20] John 3:16
[21] See John 17:3, for example.

7

unbelievers in the Bible,[22] so also, God speaks to unbelievers today. For example, during the Summer of 2000, my children and I were flying out to California. The plane was packed out and we had to be separated. I was sitting in the back when I noticed a man talking to my teenage daughter. Immediately I thought that he was hitting on her. The flight attendant must have known what I was thinking, because she invited me to move up and sit by my daughter. I plopped myself right down between them. I began to talk to the man seated next to me, who, much to my surprise, was a very nice man. He began to share with me about his business in stocks and bonds.[23] We chatted about his line of work for an hour or so, until he asked me what I did for a living.

"We move in the prophetic," I responded.

His eyes bugged out and I could see big question marks on his forehead. So I explained what the prophetic meant. Then I asked him if I could pray for him.

He said, "Sure."

I asked, "What religion are you?"

He said, "I'm Jewish."

I thought, *Oh boy, Lord, I really need your help.* For over fifteen minutes I prophesied to him. When I got done, he was amazed at the accuracy of the word. God moved mightily and spoke to a man who was not a believer in the Messiah, because God desires to love on His creation.

---

[22] E.g., 1 Kings 14:1-16, 20:13-14, Isaiah 7:3-14+

[23] I felt some rapport because, of course, Paul and Silas were into stocks and bonds. See Acts 16.

(3) The kind of word they receive:

God is deeply interested in every aspect of our lives. God has given me tens of thousands of words for people on topics as wide ranging as personal finances, self-esteem, emotional healing, marriage, family, child rearing, work, business, ministry, health, relationships with man and God, and personal character. Blue-collar prophecy not only encourages God's people to follow through on important spiritual exercises such as prayer, Bible study, worship and evangelism, but it also covers every practical issue in this life. Because God is concerned about the whole person, blue-collar prophecy addresses matters that relate to whatever situations we face in life. Pastor Tom Flaherty of Minnesota says this type of prophetic is like reading Proverbs -- God gives wisdom and practical advice that will change you in your every day activities.

(4) The method given:

Most prophecies that I heard in the 1970's and 1980's were spoken in the language of King James English. At that time, most people who prophesied read the King James Bible. However, I believe God wants to speak to his people in the language of common people.

"Thus saith the Lord," sounds impressive, but I don't recommend saying it. Instead, I encourage blue-collar prophets to use language that people can understand and relate to. The purpose of the prophetic message is not to get us to admire the eloquence of the prophet, but to hear the voice of God. We are not trying to draw attention to ourselves. Rather, we want to glorify God and get His message across.

Blue-collar prophecy also uses humor, metaphors and illustrations that relate to the person you are trying to share with. God uses sports illustrations to speak to athletes, fishing illustrations to minister to outdoorsmen, or motorcycle illustrations to relate to bikers.

Most of the prophetic meetings I have attended are intense, and for good reason: We need to passionately seek God. But, at times, God may want to share a gentle, light-hearted word to encourage us. In July 2001, I had the opportunity to minister in Pastor Shane Holden's Church. The first service was very different, most of the prophetic words were light, humorous and enjoyable. I felt I had to apologize to the Pastor. The whole night I seemed to be giddy. As I attempted to apologize to Pastor Shane and his staff, one of his staff members mentioned that tonight's service was like sitting in God's living room and Papa God was sharing funny stories with his children sitting on his knees. What a picture of how the Father is intimately concerned with every one of us!

(5) The timing of the prophetic:

Most prophetic ministries release their prophetic anointing in conferences and church services. But the blue-collar prophet is prepared to hear from God whenever and wherever He may speak -- at work, school, home, while traveling, during times with family and friends. God desires to speak to people on a daily basis. When our faith is stirred up, we will look for opportunities for God to speak through us.

One weekend I was going for a walk and I saw several junior high school kids playing basketball.

My wife asked, "Can you beat those kids in basketball?"

Male pride rose up in me. "Sure," I said. So I walked over, challenged them to a game, played, sweated, worked hard, huffed and puffed, and nearly lost my breath. But I did win -- by one point.

Meanwhile, my wife didn't even watch. Instead, she was more focused on witnessing to someone.

As I walked back over to her, exhausted but victorious, she said to me, "Why don't you give this guy a word?"

At that point, I could barely speak a word of my own, much less give one from God. Nevertheless, I sat down and did the best I could. "I see you running from God," I said, and he had been a backslider. "I see you as a good father," and, sure enough, he had custody of his kids as a single dad, something that doesn't often happen.

Then I said, "I see you becoming a Captain in the U.S. Army."

When I said that, his jaw dropped and his eyes popped open. He reached into his wallet and pulled out what looked like a driver's license. When I looked more closely, I saw that it was a military ID. He *was* a captain in the U.S. Army.

At this point, he knew it was real. He gave his life to Jesus, and went from there telling all his friends what God had done.

"Cracked pots" and the plan of God

The Bible says, *"But we have this treasure in jars of clay to show that this all-surpassing power is from God and not from us."*[24] The phrase "jars of clay"[25] actually means "cracked pots." God stores His treasures in cracked

---

[24] 2 Corinthians 4:7
[25] "Earthen vessels" in the KJV

pots like you and me so that He and only He will get the glory.

Throughout the Bible, God used all kinds of people in all kinds of ways to convey His prophetic message. He generously gifted the Corinthian church[26] even though the believers in Corinth had a lot of growing up to do.[27] God spoke through false prophets,[28] through the man who plotted the death of Jesus Christ.[29] One prophet ran away,[30] and at least three prayed to die.[31] One prophet proved a point by walking around half-naked.[32] God spoke prophecies through a backslidden king who eventually resorted to sorcery.[33] Another prophet married a prostitute.[34] Another had an affair.[35] God even spoke through an animal.[36]

As you can see, blue-collar prophecy is not just for the "marines" of Christianity. It is for every believer who has a heart to serve God, yet understands his own personal weaknesses.

Elisha, the Blue-Collar Prophet

I have chosen to use Elisha[37] the prophet as a

---

[26] 1 Corinthians 1:6-7
[27] 1 Corinthians 3:3
[28] E.g., Numbers 23:19-20
[29] John 11:50
[30] Jonah 1:3
[31] Numbers 11:15, 1 Kings 19:4, Jonah 4:3
[32] Isaiah 20:2-3
[33] 1 Samuel 19:4, 28:5-10
[34] Hosea 1:2
[35] 1 Samuel 11:2-4
[36] Numbers 22:28-30
[37] Elisha means "God saves."

Biblical model of a blue-collar prophet. His life is a wonderful living word picture of the theme of this book.

Elisha was not raised in a preacher's home nor the home of a priest. Elisha was raised as a farmer.[38] I have lived in a farming community. Farmers are (no pun intended) down-to-earth people. They know how to work with their hands. They understand what it is like to put in a full day's work. Farmers take risks; they understand that at any moment a storm or a disease can destroy years of work. Rarely do you meet a farmer who has an attitude of superiority. They understand how quickly a downturn in a market can affect their life. In a sense, a farmer's success is totally beyond his control.

Likewise, Elisha understood that God is in control. He lived with people during times of famine. He was with the army of God when they were in the desert and they ran out of water. He was familiar with suffering. He didn't live in a king's palace. He was an ordinary person like you and me. Too often our heroes in the faith live in isolated palaces with armed guards and unlisted phone numbers.[39] Yet Elisha lived with the people he loved and cared for. I pray his life will come alive once again as you read the pages of this book.

Blue-collar prophets hear the voice of God because they live with people, understand people, and can feel the heartbeat of people. As a result, they share a message that is relatable, applicable and life-changing.

---

[38] 1 Kings 19:19
[39] Sometimes they have good reasons for these protective measures, as you will read later on.

CHAPTER 2:

Stories from the Life of Elisha, the Blue-Collar Prophet

God wants to draw unbelievers to you, so you can give them a message from Him.

I visit and speak in churches all over North America. One time, in South Dakota, after a church service, we were getting ready to go out to eat.

My son was traveling with me. He asked, "If the pastor asks us where do you want to go out to eat, what are you going to tell him?"

As a rule, I never ask a pastor where we can go eat or tell him I'd like to go here or there. If he asks, I say, "Well, where do you want to go?"

But, this time, I said to my son, "If he asks me, I'll say, 'Red Lobster.'"

Sure enough, as soon as we got into the car, the pastor asked, "Where do you want to go out to eat?"

"Red Lobster," I answered.

Since I normally would never suggest a restaurant, I felt bad about saying it. But the pastor said, "Great, that's where we want to go."

When we got there, I wasn't thinking about gifts of the Spirit. I was thinking about Calamari, and about shrimp. My agenda was food, but God had something better planned.

Our waiter was a large man -- big, strong, and tall. We learned that he had, at one time, tried out for professional basketball. When he came to the table, God began to feed me words for him.

He is running from God. He has a mother who is praying for him. He has had a broken heart.

When he came to our table, I just passed God's message on to our waiter. Pretty soon he couldn't stay away. He served another table, and ran right back to ours. He stood there listening, with tears in his eyes. God began to give him one word after another. It was powerful.

Breaking barriers to get results that last

For fifteen years I taught witnessing by going door to door. I knocked at the door and said, "I am not a Jehovah's Witness, I'm not from the Mafia, and I am not going to sell you anything. May I take a brief survey?" Most people agreed to the survey, I shared the gospel, and many people made a decision for Christ.

Here's the problem: I got decisions, not disciples. I'm not the only one who has faced this challenge. I spoke with one evangelist who organized teams of hundreds of Christians, got tens of thousands of people saved every year, but couldn't think of a single person who had been added to the church as a result of his ministry.

Jesus said to make disciples,[40] not get decisions.

When Jesus sent His disciples door-to-door, He didn't ask them to conduct surveys. He gave them power to drive out evil spirits and to heal diseases.[41] I found out why

---

[40]   Matthew 28:19
[41]   Matthew 10:1 - see also 1 Corinthians 2:4-5

when the Lord began to use me in the prophetic and in some of the other supernatural gifts of the Spirit. When people experience supernatural revelation through the gifts of the Spirit, when people are instantaneously healed, they remember their experience with God. Their decisions "stick," and, years later, they are still serving God.[42] I have taught over 500 evangelism training seminars from coast to coast. I have written textbooks on evangelism, one of which is used at the college level. But moving in the prophetic represents a paradigm shift for me, that brought a whole new level of effectiveness to my evangelistic ministry.

For example, in 1998 I was in Seattle when two Mormons knocked on the door of the home I was staying in. For the next two hours I used my old method of debating. I was enjoying myself as I proved them wrong time and time again, using the book of Mormon to do it. After they left, I said to God, "God, what do you think? Pretty good, huh?"

The Lord's answer cut to the heart of the issue. *Is that the way I taught you how to witness?*

"No," I had to admit.

God sternly spoke to me. *Don't do that any more. Don't hammer people.*

I realized then that I had I won the argument, but I lost the opportunity to share Jesus Christ with two people who needed Him.

Thank God, He soon gave me another opportunity.

---

[42] Of course, some people don't follow through no matter what method of evangelism you use. The point is, we've seen more lasting results with the prophetic.

That night I went out to eat with a group of people. The waiter was a Mormon. I asked if I could pray for him. Within a few minutes God gave me three bits of information that were very specific and relevant to this young man's life. I saw family problems. I saw issues with his parents.

Then I asked, "Do you want to give your life to Jesus?"

He prayed right there to receive the Lord.

Then the Lord said to me, *Now that's how I want you to witness. Use your prophetic anointing.*

That prophetic anointing can be powerful in the life of an unbeliever. Paul writes:

> *But if an unbeliever or someone who does not understand comes in while everybody is prophesying, he will be convinced by all that he is a sinner and will be judged by all, and the secrets of his heart will be laid bare. So he will fall down and worship God, exclaiming, "God is really among you!"* [43]

This Scripture was written to a multi-cultural society that had dozens of different religions to choose from. How were the Corinthians supposed to prove that Jesus was the only way? Biblical facts are convincing to believers, but sometimes unbelievers need more than Bible

---

[43] 1 Corinthians 14:24-25

proof texts, they need supernatural signs and wonders.[44]

Jesus ran into a similar challenge when he stopped at a well, thirsty after a long walk on a hot, dry day. At that moment He found Himself with an opportunity to share the gospel with a Samaritan woman. But he had to overcome all kinds of barriers. He needed to break through ethnic hatred, gender separation, and the walls put up by her sinful lifestyle. How did He do it? Jesus used His prophetic gift to reveal details about her failures in marriage. Even though she tried to throw Him off, His prophetic word hooked her, and brought her to the belief that He was the Messiah. As a result, one of the greatest revivals in the gospels began.[45]

A number of years ago I shared my faith with an atheist who was extremely intelligent and fairly wealthy. I started with the approach I described in my textbook, *Learning How to Share Your Faith*. The book contains a whole chapter on how to talk to atheists. I tried my best using this approach, all to no avail. Then I began to pray for him. Although I knew some of his personal problems, God revealed two details that only he and one other person knew.

"How did you know that?" he wanted to know. "Only one other person knows that information."

I explained to him that God Almighty just demonstrated that He was real. Minutes later this avowed atheist became a believer.

My wife loves witnessing to people on the Internet.

---

[44] 1 Corinthians 2:4
[45] John 4:4-42

One day she entered a chat room, "Satanism vs. Christianity." The Christians were trying to preach to the Satanists, quoting the Bible. The Satanists were swearing and mocking us. We began to reach out to one of them, and we went into a private chat room to talk.

His name was Reverend So-and-so -- whatever that meant -- some reverend demon thing. We started to chat, and God gave me prophetic words for him.

I shared the word "abortion."

"Yeah," he admitted, "we've had one."

God gave me the word "sexual perversion."

Again he admitted that the word applied.

God told me that something bad happened seven years earlier.

Again, he admitted we were right, but he wasn't going to tell us what happened.

He tried to divert the conversation into a debate about Christianity and doctrine, but God nailed him on very specific words -- words he couldn't deny.

Throughout Scripture, God used the prophetic and other supernatural gifts of the Spirit to win souls. Elisha evangelized Namaan through healing.[46] God used a prophetic word from Daniel to get Nebuchadnezzar to acknowledge the Most High God.[47] Philip was prompted to witness to the Ethiopian eunuch through a prophetic word.[48] Jonah had a prophetic word and a whole nation repented.[49] The use of signs and wonders was tied to the

---

[46] 2 Kings 5:1-19
[47] Daniel 4
[48] Acts 8:26-40
[49] Jonah 3:1-10

Great Commission in Mark's Gospel.[50]

Evangelism is close to the heart of God. God wants to give you the tools you need -- that is, spiritual gifts -- to win people to Christ.

Sometimes, you may use these gifts inside the church. More often, however, you will prophesy in your daily life -- in your work place, at home, in the secular world.

These "power gifts" like prophecy, word of knowledge, word of wisdom, healing, miracles, and faith work hand in hand with the more "quiet" gifts, for example, the gift of helps. In fact, part of the ministry of prophetic evangelism is to raise up people who will go into the community and do good works (i.e., use the gift of helps). God will raise up people to pass out cookies door to door, volunteer in a food pantry, give away clothing, or paint a widow's home.

The result? Christ is lifted up and people are drawn to Him. Jesus put it this way: "In the same way, let your light shine before men, that they may see your good deeds and praise your Father in heaven."[51]

Elisha used the gift of healing to evangelize the pagan Naaman. Naaman was commander of the army of Aram, an often-hostile nation near the border of Israel. His servant girl, an Israelite captured during a raid, urged Naaman to visit Elisha to be healed of his leprosy. After some detours and delays, Naaman was healed by following

---

[50]   Mark 16:15-18
[51]   Matthew 5:16

21

the prophet's instruction to bathe seven times in the Jordan River.[52] The story picks up in 2 Kings 5:

> *15 Then Naaman and all his attendants went back to the man of God. He stood before him and said, "Now I know that there is no God in all the world except in Israel. Please accept now a gift from your servant."*
>
> *16 The prophet answered, "As surely as the Lord lives, whom I serve, I will not accept a thing." And even though Naaman urged him, he refused.*
>
> *17 "If you will not," said Naaman, "please let me, your servant, be given as much earth as a pair of mules can carry, for your servant will never again make burnt offerings and sacrifices to any other god but the Lord . 18 But may the Lord forgive your servant for this one thing: When my master enters the temple of Rimmon to bow down and he is leaning on my arm and I bow there also-when I bow down in the temple of Rimmon, may the Lord forgive your servant for this."*
>
> *19 "Go in peace," Elisha said.*

Healing the brokenhearted

For nine years I traveled all across North America

---

[52] 2 Kings 5:1-14

conducting over 500 personal evangelism seminars. I worked hard, but there was little tangible fruit. In 1996 the Lord showed me that the church was like Peter's mother-in-law[53]. She was sick, but when Jesus healed her, she got up and ministered back to Jesus. The church family has been rocked with rejection, persecution, family problems and serious emotional wounds, but when the anointing comes from Jesus there begins a healing process that heals people from the core.

One of the key purposes of the prophetic is found in this powerful axiom: What God reveals he heals. As the Lord begins to reveal the pains and emotional scars in a person's past or present situation, the healing balm of Gilead is released into a person's heart. In prophecy the heart of God is manifested and He begins to heal the pain in the bride's heart.

Dozens and dozens of times God has revealed physical, emotional and sexual abuse. As these sensitive areas are exposed, the wounded victim begins to understand that God was there all the time. Even though people have buried their past, it is like a deadly undetected infection that is spreading throughout a person's soul, devouring and destroying all of the potential that God has placed in that person. Just as a doctor or chiropractor or psychologist will dig into a person to find the root cause, so will the Lord Jesus penetrate the thick calloused scars in a person's soul, so he can uproot the deadly poison and restore the believer to a position of wholeness.

---

[53] See Matthew 8:14-15

God wants to speak words of comfort and encouragement through you.

I pray for 10,000 people a year. As I pray for them, God gives me words for them - supernaturally revealed words from God. He wants to do the same for you.

For example, one night I was praying over a man and the Lord told me to ask, "Why is your heart breaking?" The man explained that his wife was leaving him. But I was able to give him hope from the Lord that he would recover.

When I started praying for the next man, the Lord said, "Ask him, 'What are you trying to prove?'" The Lord showed me that there was a little boy inside him trying to be good enough for a dad that was impossible to please. Then I was able to give this man a word from the Lord, "I love you just the way you are." It was clear from his tears that this man was deeply moved.

Then I prayed for a woman. The Lord showed me that she was "singing a sad song." He revealed to me that she was tormented by a spirit of shame. The Lord gave me the anointing to break the power of that evil spirit over her.

God went on that evening to identify through me broken marriages, wounded childhoods, spiritual backsliding and need -- and to set into motion healing, deliverance, salvation and recovery. The Lord wants to speak the same kinds of powerful, encouraging, life-changing words through you to people God will bring to you.

Over and over again I have seen people who have been destroyed through divorce, incest, rejection and church splits. But God brings healing and hope through the gifts of the Spirit. Through the prophetic, God may use you to reveal depression and oppression, and pray an anointed prayer that breaks the yoke of bondage for someone else. God wants to release His children into joy.[54]

Many of God's people are like Gideon, sincere, committed, but paralyzed with fear and discouragement. God gave Gideon a whole new self image, a new sense of identity when He called him "a mighty warrior."[55] In the same way, God wants to use you to speak new paradigms into the lives of His people.

A spirit of condemnation had stripped me of confidence in my calling, but a pastor stated that I really was a man of love as evidenced by the hours and hours of praying for people. This word so encouraged me that I not only continued on in my ministry, but I resolved to fight even harder for the Lord.

True prophets are designed by the Father to make ready a people that will glorify the King of kings.[56] The Spirit of Christ makes us ready by producing the fruit of righteousness in us. As Scripture says:

> *But the fruit of the Spirit is love, joy, peace, patience, kindness, goodness, faithfulness, gentleness and self-control. Against such things there is no law.*[57]

The prophetic word gives us practical insight on how to *love* one another. It produces *joy* as God begins to

---

[54] Isaiah 64:3
[55] Judges 6:12
[56] Luke 1:17
[57] Galatians 5:22-23

heal our past and give us hope for the future. His rich prophetic anointing causes inner *peace* as we realize that God knows every detail in our lives and therefore we can trust him to lead and guide us. As the gift of prophecy is released we are forced to wait expectantly, but *patiently* as God begins to unfold his perfect will for our lives. I have found that prophecy causes the church to begin to reach out to the lost and to the body of Christ with practical demonstration of the *goodness* and *kindness* of Christ which causes the lost to repent and the body to bond together. In the body of Christ, the secular workplace and the family there is such a lack of faithfulness that whole companies, churches and families are immobilized. But the spirit of prophecy encourages us to be *faithful* in the small things to prepare us for future acts of obedience that will release into a deeper level of responsibility. The word of prophecy brings healing and deliverance from anger, hostility and bitterness resulting in a spirit of meekness and *gentleness* that causes hard-core people to melt with the love of Christ. Finally, the prophetic word causes us to grow in *self-control* as the weaknesses of the flesh are confronted and dealt with so nothing is hidden from the convicting and delivering power of the Holy Spirit.

Golf, oil and Allen wrenches -- God's creative ways of restoring and preserving families

A man came forward for prayer one time when I was in Des Moines, Iowa. He was divorced and I could see that he was at that time in a bad relationship. I saw a couple of things that were right on about his then-current situation. Then I saw the word "golf."

We couldn't make sense out of it. He didn't play golf. He had never played golf. So, like a lot of other words that don't make sense, we just had to put it on the shelf.

But we did have a word for him that he would meet the right woman.

Later, he ended up dating a woman I happened to know from Bible school. She was divorced, just like he was. As he was dating her, he was wondering if he should marry this girl or just forget it. Then he went to stay at her brother's house. He had never been there before. During the visit, he prayed, "God show me Your will. Is this the right one?"

Then he walked into the brother's bathroom, turned on the light, and there was golf everywhere - a golf shower curtain, golf wall paper, golf towels, golf everything.

God had answered his prayer! He married this woman and today they are serving God in a worship ministry.

Families are under constant attack from the enemy. But God always has a creative way of keeping families strong and intact. Things were no different in Elisha's day. Here's an example from 2 Kings 4, of how God rescued the family of a single mom:

> *1 The wife of a man from the company of the prophets cried out to Elisha, "Your servant my husband is dead, and you know that he revered the Lord . But now his creditor is coming to take my two boys as his slaves."*
>
> *2 Elisha replied to her, "How can I help you? Tell me, what do you have in your house?"*

"Your servant has nothing there at all," she said, "except a little oil."

3 Elisha said, "Go around and ask all your neighbors for empty jars. Don't ask for just a few. 4 Then go inside and shut the door behind you and your sons. Pour oil into all the jars, and as each is filled, put it to one side."

5 She left him and afterward shut the door behind her and her sons. They brought the jars to her and she kept pouring. 6 When all the jars were full, she said to her son, "Bring me another one."

But he replied, "There is not a jar left." Then the oil stopped flowing.

7 She went and told the man of God, and he said, "Go, sell the oil and pay your debts. You and your sons can live on what is left."

Blue-collar prophecy usually includes practical, God-directed advice and counsel. Although the Bible gives clear commands and godly principles to help us make wise decisions, we sometimes need more specific explanations and direction. In this case, this widow needed to know what to do to keep her family together. She needed a word of wisdom from the Lord. In another situation, Elisha told the woman whose son was restored to life to "Go away with your family and stay for a while wherever you can, because the Lord has decreed a famine in the land that will last seven years[58]."

Sometimes, God's children just need to know that God knows and cares about the troubles they are going through. I prayed for a man recently in Wisconsin and I saw his wife being unfaithful . This man loved his kids with all his heart. Then I saw a picture of an Allen wrench. I told him I saw a picture of an Allen wrench. "Do you know anybody named Allen?" I asked.

"Yeah," he said, "my son."

As a result, he knew that God knew, that God cared, and that God would be there for him to help him love his family.

I was praying for a guy in Omaha, Nebraska, and I saw that he was to reconcile with his dad. He was to write a letter and say he was sorry. He needed to repent and make things right. Then, all of a sudden, I saw a picture of my cousin. His name is Steve. Sometimes God will allow me to see a parallel picture. I will see something I know about that relates to something in their life. I said, "I see a picture of my cousin named Steve. Do you know anybody named Steve?"

He said, "Yeah, my father."

And his mouth dropped open and he knew it was God. And he sat in the service with his eyes wide open like silver dollars. *Wow, God knows the name of my father.* This touched him. He realized, *Yeah, I'm supposed to call my dad. I'm supposed to make things right.*

---

[58] 2 Kings 8:1

Cleanup time

In the Law of Moses, the Israelites were told that touching an unclean thing or an unclean person would make them unholy, or unclean. Eating unclean food would make them unholy[59]. But when Jesus arrived, He introduced an entirely new paradigm. He touched people who were dirty and He made them clean[60]. In the same way, God has called us to touch an unholy world and bring cleansing from above.

God used Elisha to bring cleansing to the environment. Through the prophet, God cleaned up a toxic spring. We read in 2 Kings 2:

> 19 The men of the city said to Elisha, "Look, our lord, this town is well situated, as you can see, but the water is bad and the land is unproductive."
>
> 20 "Bring me a new bowl," he said, "and put salt in it." So they brought it to him.
>
> 21 Then he went out to the spring and threw the salt into it, saying, "This is what the Lord says: 'I have healed this water. Never again will it cause death or make the land unproductive.' " 22 And the water has remained wholesome to this day, according to the word Elisha had spoken.

God cares about restoring the environment.

---

[59] See, e.g., Leviticus 11 & 15
[60] E.g., Luke 12:12-13

Sometimes Christians are branded as world-denying ascetics uninterested in the environment and the universe God created. But, in fact, the opposite should be true. Because sin is responsible for the destruction of the environment[61], only God and His people can turn that around.

The people of Jericho asked Elisha for help. When was the last time the world consulted the church and asked for help?

Elisha threw the salt into a polluted spring. That's where we need to be -- someplace where we can bring healing.

Of course, God is interested in more than just the environment. He wants to purify more than water; He wants to purify the bride of Christ. Sometimes He does this by confronting sin. Like Nathan who was called upon to confront David, sometimes God will use blue-collar prophets to point out sins like bitterness, adultery, lying, divisiveness, criticalness, addictive behavior, backbiting and so on. When this happens the fear of God comes upon the church and upon unbelievers[62].

Sometimes God wants to purify core beliefs. For example, I prayed for one fellow who appeared to me to be Hispanic. His wife was Caucasian. As the Lord gave me words about their marriage, she was crying, which is a good sign that the words were right on. When I prayed over him, I saw the star of David. I also saw the word "racist." In the

---

[61] See, e.g., Numbers 35:33, Ezra 9:11, Amos 4:6-10, Joel 1:2-12, Jeremiah 12:10-13

[62] Acts 5:1-9, 1 Corinthians 14:24-25

natural, I was thinking *Hispanics aren't racist against Jews.* So the word didn't make much sense to me. When I told the man what I saw, he looked at me and didn't make a comment. So I just went on.

But later, as I was walking out of church, he came up to me and asked me how I knew all those things. I said, "God knows them. I don't know them. Jesus told me."

He said, "Oh."

A couple minutes later the man who invited this couple to church came over and spoke with me as I was getting ready to get in my car. He informed me that the man I thought was Hispanic was not Hispanic at all. He was Muslim.

Suddenly, the prophecy made sense. God was at work to purify this man's core beliefs, to root out his racism toward Jews.

Sometimes you will encounter people who have been involved in demonic activity. One time, a lady came to one of our meetings and said, with a very sarcastic voice, "Praise the Lord, praise the Lord." I discerned it was demonic. She was a minister in another "borderline" denomination. We prayed deliverance for her. God purified her.

Deliverance in the desert

Dry times happen to all of us. But God often uses the prophetic to get the river of God's Spirit flowing again. In 2 Kings 3, Elisha was called upon to get the king of Israel, the king of Judah and their armies out of a terrible predicament. They had marched through the desert to attack the country of Moab. Along the way, they ran out of water, and death threatened them before they even reached

Moab. God gave Elisha a word of wisdom on how to handle the problem.

"Dig ditches[63]," Elisha instructed. When they did so, God filled the ditches with water. Strengthened by that water and by a word from the Lord, Israel's armies went on to win the victory.

I ministered in a church in Iowa. My wife, four of our children, and my brother-in-law came along, and we all stayed with the pastor and his wife in their two-bedroom house. On our way to church we drove by this beautiful church. It was gorgeous. The pastor said, "See that beautiful church?"

I said, "That's a pretty church."

The pastor said, "That's not mine. Mine's the dump next to it."

And he was right. It was a dump. Part of the floor was actually caving in. The pastor was a really nice brother, but they didn't have a piano player and so he led worship playing the piano with one finger. It was pretty bad.

Eight people showed up at church, so we literally doubled the church that week.

The service was dry and I was praying that somehow God would get me out of there. And my wife leaned over and said, "You'd better preach as though there's a thousand people here." And so, I was convicted by my wife and the Holy Spirit together.

And so, I gave it all my heart.

A lady came up and I prayed for her and she got

---

[63] 2 Kings 3:16-17

touched.

That night another church came and there were about 40 people.

That lady who came in the morning brought a friend. When I prayed for that friend, I saw a rope around her neck in the Spirit. I learned that she, in fact, wanted to die. She was planning her suicide that week.

As a result of the prophetic, she decided to live. She got saved, she got delivered. She brought her daughter to church. Her daughter got saved. And then her daughter brought a friend to church. That little church probably had 65-70 visitors in a three day period.

Even though things started out dry, lives were saved -- not just spiritually, but physically. God showed up.

On another occasion, I was on vacation in northern Minnesota, way up north where the men are men, and so are the women. I stopped in a church, not to minister, but as a visitor. The service was very dry and boring. The pastor was trying to get people pumped up, but nobody got excited.

The pastor had people shake hands. A guy shook my hand and God told me he had a spirit of poverty. I thought, that's interesting. And then the pastor started preaching. All of a sudden, my back started hurting. That's usually a sign that somebody in the church had a back problem. And the specific word was, they hurt it at work. And I couldn't share it. I'm just a guest. I'm not even supposed to preach. I'm on vacation. And I could just see in the spirit realm that God's hands were being tied. There's nothing He could do. The pastor wanted God to do something, but nobody believed the Lord was going to do anything special.

After the pastor preached, he gave an altar call for salvation. Nobody came up. He asked if anybody wanted to be filled with the Holy Spirit. Nobody came up. He asked if anybody wanted to be healed. Nobody came up. He was giving it his best shot.

Then he said, "We have a guest preacher in town. Let's pray for him." I knew that was an open door. So I walked up to the pastor and said, "I believe someone here hurt themselves at work, they hurt their back and they need to be healed. Is there anybody here like that I could pray for?"

A man raised his hand. The pastor said I could pray for him.

The guy with the curse of poverty came up. I prayed for him and God touched him.

I said, "There's somebody here who has migraine headaches. God wants to heal them." A lady came up. God touched her.

I said, "Pastor, you need prayer." I prayed for him.

I looked at his wife. I said, "You need prayer." She started crying. I prayed for her.

I saw someone in the audience and said, "You need to be filled with the Holy Spirit." She came up and got filled with the Holy Spirit.

There were 35 people lined up to get prayed for.

As I walked out, people walked up to me and said, "How did you know that? How did you know that?"

Nobody knew who I was. I'm sure they asked, "Who was that masked man?"

Things were dry. But God showed up.

Remove the poison!

Sometimes poison needs to be removed from the

35

church for it to function the way God intended.

I was with one pastor. And I just had this weird feeling about him. He was talking on the phone with a lady. I said, "Who is that?"

He answered, "Oh, it's somebody from the church."

And I asked him, "Are you committing adultery?"

He never answered me. Later he admitted that he was having an affair. He resigned from the church. God uncovered the poison and cleaned out the church.

God used Elisha to remove literal poison from a stew in 2 Kings 4:

> *38 Elisha returned to Gilgal and there was a famine in that region. While the company of the prophets was meeting with him, he said to his servant, "Put on the large pot and cook some stew for these men."*
>
> *39 One of them went out into the fields to gather herbs and found a wild vine. He gathered some of its gourds and filled the fold of his cloak. When he returned, he cut them up into the pot of stew, though no one knew what they were. 40 The stew was poured out for the men, but as they began to eat it, they cried out, "O man of God, there is death in the pot!" And they could not eat it.*
>
> *41 Elisha said, "Get some flour." He put it into the pot and said, "Serve it to the people to eat." And there was nothing harmful in the pot.*

Some things seem innocuous on the surface, but underneath they are poisonous. We've had psychics come to our meetings. We've had people who have had ungodly intentions come to the meetings, and they've been exposed. One guy came up to me, and I saw "lack of integrity." Here he was a con man. He had been in trouble for bilking ladies out of their money. He was discovered, but he had still caused a lot of damage.

The very first time I conducted a revival, I received a word of knowledge, and God used it to remove poison from the church. I was presenting a seminar in Iowa in 1996. At lunchtime, the pastor said to me, "What did you think of worship?"

I said, "Well, it wasn't very anointed, to be honest with you."

He said, "I think my worship director might be in trouble with the law."

I said, "Why, is he molesting his son?"

This worship director was accused of molesting his son. They removed him that day. I think he ended up going to jail. The church was cleansed. They had over a hundred visitors in two weeks. People were healed, delivered, and set free of demons. That was the first revival I had ever been to in my life. Revival came because of a word of knowledge.

Demonic games in the church basement

I was in a church in Minnesota, and the pastor was wondering why his worship wasn't flowing. It seemed "plugged up" and he couldn't understand why. They were crying out to God over why the worship wasn't flowing. I started praying for some of the kids and, in the Spirit, I saw them playing devil games in the basement of the church. We cast demons out of three of the church member's kids -- demons that got established because they were doing demonic games in the basement of the church. And as they repented and we cleansed it, a new worship came the next week. Poisonous stew was healed, and they experienced true worship.

Pull out the evil roots

Many people are in bondage to sin, the flesh and the devil. When the prophetic begins to flow people begin to get set free. Sometimes people are bound by sin and the fruit of the sin is evident to all, but the roots of the sin are buried. For instance a person may have an anger problem, but the prophetic will reveal the root problem as a generational curse, unforgiveness, demonism, lack of sleep or whatever. The best way to destroy evil fruit is to pull out evil roots. Jesus spent a lot of time dealing with demonic forces. One woman came to him that was described as a daughter of Abraham. She was hunched over. Jesus discerned it was an evil spirit and then he cast out the spirit and the woman was delivered and healed. If a person needs a deliverance from demonic powers, it is essential to operate in the prophetic to find out which demonic entity is controlling the person. Jesus asked the evil spirit within the demoniac, "What is your name?" When the name of the demon was stated the demon was instantly cast out. A good doctor doesn't just study symptoms but he tries to get to the root of the problem. The prophetic can get to the root of the problem with one word. The prophetic word will also give solutions that will free people from slavery and addictions.

Get rid of controlling spirits

Jezebel, the wife of King Ahab, caused incredible damage to ancient Israel. She introduced Baal worship[64], killed the Lord's prophets[65], promoted Asherah worship[66], threatened to kill Elijah[67], and arranged the murder of Naboth[68]. Ahab was king, but Jezebel ran the show. As such, she serves as a type for controlling spirits that create problems today. Just as the Lord used Jehu to remove Jezebel[69], so also, the Lord may use you to remove controlling spirits from the lives of people.

One time in Canada I prayed over a lady who was holding a four-year-old child. This child was one of the most unruly children I have ever seen. When her mom held her, she pulled her mom's hair. When her dad held her, she pulled her dad's hair. They attempted to restrain her, and then she pulled her own hair. Through the prophetic, I saw that this child had a spirit of rejection. That was the root cause for her misbehavior. The child's mother later told me that after her daughter was conceived, the doctor told her to abort the baby. The mom considered it for a long time, but finally decided to forego the abortion. Even so, a spirit of rejection had been installed in this child's life even before she was born. She felt rejected and kept trying to hurt herself. Just as Jezebel had a murderous spirit, so also this evil spirit sought to destroy this family and this child's life.

---

[64] 1 Kings 16:31
[65] 1 Kings 18:4, 13
[66] 1 Kings 18:19
[67] 1 Kings 19:1-2
[68] 1 Kings 21:7-15
[69] 2 Kings 9:30-37

We set up a time and I prayed deliverance over this little girl. I had to hold both arms, she was squirming and screaming, but all of a sudden she threw up, and then she was as calm as a brand new little puppy dog -- just calm, sweet and huggable. This little four-year-old girl then came to our kids crusade; she totally behaved even though she had never behaved that well before. The spirit of Jezebel, that controlling spirit, was cast out. The little girl was set free, and her whole life was changed.

Haunting thoughts

I was talking to a man, and I saw "haunting thoughts." I asked him, "Is something haunting you?" As I asked him that question, and gave him a chance to respond, God said, "Whatever he says, that's not what I want to deal with. It's the second thing that he's going to bring up."

He began by talking about the death of his dad. And it was true. These were haunting thoughts.

I said, "But there's something deeper than that." I paused and added, "Is it private?"

He said, "Yeah." So I brought him off to the side. He told me that he had been in a relationship with another guy for a number of years. The first answer was a true answer, but it wasn't what God was trying to deal with. He was trying to deal with this ungodly, unhealthy relationship that happened 10 years ago.

Even though he had repented and God had forgiven him, he still felt guilty about it. These thoughts came back. God had forgiven and forgotten his sin. But, because the devil kept condemning him, God brought it up to get rid of these thoughts of condemnation, this controlling spirit from the devil, this root of Jezebel. This man went away set free, knowing that God had forgiven him.

Ashes to beauty

The devil loves to steal. He loves to steal our health. He loves to steal our family. He loves to steal our finances. He loves to steal our ministry. He loves to steal our hope, our dreams. Many times the prophetic will restore what the enemy took. It will restore dreams. For example, I'll pray over people and I'll see "singing" and they quit singing years ago -- or I'll see "artistic skills" and they quit painting years ago. I see them in a business, and they used to dream about being in a business. God restores a dream that died. Other people have been divorced and I see a marriage reconciled, or I see them getting remarried to someone. Other people have "lost" their children, and I encourage them to make a new effort with their child. "Start calling your child. Start reaching out to him. Try to build that relationship with her again." Others have lost finances, or have lost their business, and then God will give them a prophetic word to restart their business. They've lost a house, and God will give them a word that they are going to get a new house. Some have lost their ministry, but God wants to restore them. I remember praying for a guy in Wisconsin. He went through a divorce and lost his ministry. Through me God told him that He was going to restore him. I believe the day is coming when he will be brought back into ministry. God is continually restoring what the devil stole.

God is in the business of restoring what the enemy has taken. When one of the prophets lost the iron axhead in the Jordan River, God used Elisha to miraculously restore property[70]. When Naaman the Aramean lost his flesh to leprosy, God gave Elisha the word of wisdom that restored Naaman's health[71]. When the Israelites resorted to cannibalism during the siege of Samaria, God used Elisha to free the city and restore their hope[72]. When the Shunammite family returned to Israel after a famine forced their exile, God restored their livelihood[73]. And when the miracle son of the the Shunammite couple suddenly fell dead during harvest, God used the prophet Elisha to restore his life[74].

If the devil has taken something from you, you can believe that God is going to restore it. And God will give you words for people about restoration that will stir their faith and hope.

Restoring health

One of the blessings of traveling is meeting some of God's hidden warriors who have learned truths in areas that you have no experience. Such is the case with an anointed couple named Eugene and Pearl Werner. I have been blessed to know this sweet couple from mid-state Wisconsin. They have been flowing in a healing anointing similar to Charles and Francis Hunter.

One day brother Eugene shared with me a concept called sympathetic pain. He explained that God will allow him to feel pain in a certain part of his body. This was a sign to him that someone in the audience had that same

---

[70] 2 Kings 6:1-7
[71] 2 Kings 5:1-19
[72] 2 Kings 6:24-7:20
[73] 2 Kings 8:1-6
[74] 2 Kings 4:18-37

pain. God instructed him that if he would call out the pain in faith, the Lord would honor that step and heal the person. I have seen this work 100's of times. I recall driving to a church in southern Iowa and much to my chagrin my foot began to swell up so bad that I had to take my shoe off. In fact, I commented to my oldest daughter Jessica that my foot was swelling up. I then recalled what the Werner's taught me about sympathetic pain. So I made a mental note to pray for people who had swelling in their feet. I also reminded my daughter to not let me forget to pray for people with swollen feet or ankles. After preaching that night I made mention of the swelling, but no one came up. I thought , "Oh well," and I went on to praying for other people. Shortly thereafter my daughter noticed a lady who had crutches and was walking out of the service. She then asked her to come forward for prayer. The lady came forward and dropped her crutch and was instantly healed.

I have seen numerous people healed of back, stomach, elbow, shoulder, neck problems through the power of God being released through the combination of two gifts, the word of knowledge and healing. Not only are sicknesses detected through sympathetic pain, but God has given me words such as glands, fallopian tubes, gall bladder, etc. Or I will see body parts that need healing when I am praying for people.

Another way that God brings healing is through words of wisdom. One of the first words of wisdom I had was back in 1984 when I was praying for a friend of mine with a back problem, I felt inclined to ask him if he slept on his stomach. He admitted that he did. From what I know sleeping on your stomach is hard on your lower back because your muscles are tense all night long and they never get a chance to rest. When the young man changed the way he slept his back got better. Other times I have recommended herbs or juice diets. One time I felt like I should recommend to a person with bad knees that she walk up the stairs backwards. When I mentioned walking up the stairs backwards I thought it was rather strange until the lady said her chiropractor had recommended the same thing just days before. For those blue-collar prophets who get an opportunity to minister in a church setting, ask the Lord before the service which healing gift does he want to pass out. If you listen and watch carefully, God will show you what he wants to do.

Remember that healing isn't just for believers. Elisha, through a word of wisdom, brought healing to the pagan Naaman. What was the result? The result was salvation. Naaman turned to the Lord. Even though he had to return to his pagan culture, he went with the blessing of God. What better way to share the gospel! Heal the physical man, so Christ can heal the whole man.

"Go in peace."

Naaman returned to the pagan temple, but Elisha said, "Go in peace." I've had Mormons come to my meetings three or four years in a row. Every word I've had for them has been accurate. It's helped them in their faith. They've given their lives to Christ. This goes against my theology. They're still Mormons, but they've given their lives to Christ and they love Jesus. They love what we do, and they support our ministry. It sounds crazy.

Naaman was healed, but he still worshipped in the false temple, even though he was a believer in the true God. "I'm really worshipping the true God even though I'm in the false temple," and Elisha, *the* prophet, never said a word - he seemed to say, "That's okay." God didn't have a problem with it because he saw the man's heart.

Restoring ministry and confirming words

I met a builder who was a former minister. He had a large church, but things didn't work out with his marriage. So he ended up quitting the ministry and starting a very successful construction company. When I described the prophetic to him, it didn't make much sense because of the denominational background from which he came. One day, on my way to meet with him, I prayed, "Lord, give me a word for him." And I thought the Lord said, "I'm going to restore his ministry."

When I reached his home, I told him, "God has a word for you."

He said, "What's that?" This man has several degrees. He's very intelligent, very sharp.

I said, "God's going to restore your ministry." And he looked at me, and his mouth dropped open, and he hit the table and said, "I thought about that on the way here. On the way here, I felt the Lord tell me that I was going to be restored in the ministry."

God confirmed what he was telling him. This is a key to the prophetic. Most words -- not all -- but most words are confirming words. Sometimes we're not sure how God is leading or what, exactly, God's will is for us. So a prophetic word will confirm what God is already speaking to someone.

There are many good things we can do. But we want to do the God thing. There's a difference between doing something good and doing something that is of God. The prophetic will help you discern what's good and what's of God.

When your life is taken away, God hands it back

Elisha was used by God to restore the Shunammite's son to life when he suddenly fell ill and then died during harvest[75]. His mother was overcome with grief, but she exercised faith and sought out the prophet Elisha. When Elisha heard the news, he sent his servant Gehazi to raise the boy from the dead.

It didn't work.

Elisha could have given up at this point, but he didn't. He persevered in prayer, until God unlocked the answer and restored the boy's life.

You may be used to raise someone from the dead. But even if you aren't, life is restored in other ways as well. Sometimes it seems that there's no hope. People are going no where in life. They've reached bottom. There's no purpose in life. They go into a Job experience. Then a prophetic word can inspire people and give them hope. That God has a plan for them.

This happened to a man who saw a poster advertising our meetings and decided to show up. He had a stroke. He had lost his health. Half his body wasn't working right. It was very humbling. But he and his wife showed up at our meeting and they both got saved. They came forward for prayer, and I was able to give them several prophetic words that hit home.

Then God gave me a word that just didn't make sense. I saw the word "amputee." He couldn't make sense out of the word and neither could I.

But, on his way home, God reminded him that his dad's uncle was an amputee. In World War II, his dad's

---

[75] 2 Kings 4:18-37

46

uncle was in an army tank when a mortar shell came into the tank and exploded. He was burning up and on fire. The captain wanted to shoot him. He said, "I'm going to put you out of your misery." But the uncle replied, "If you shoot me, I'll never talk to you again." So the captain put out the fire, wrapped him up the best he could, and put him on the top of the tank to transport him to a ship. On the way he got shot three more times. Finally, they got on the ship, and then the ship sank. But they managed to save him, and get him on a plane. He lost his leg, but he did survive. And he did more than survive. He ended up climbing mountains, going on bike rides in the mountains, doing all kinds of things that most people with two legs can't do even though he was an amputee.

God used this powerful word picture to bring hope to this stroke victim. And, as a result, the stroke victim has gone on to remodel an entire house with his left side almost paralyzed. He is a mechanic, an inventor, a builder. And he's slowly getting back some use of his left side. This stroke could have ended his life, but God had other plans -- plans He set into motion through the prophetic.

Life restored and victory won

Eventually, even Elisha grew old, grew sick and died. But he went out with a flurry. Here's the story from 2 Kings 13:

> *14 Now Elisha was suffering from the illness from which he died. Jehoash king of Israel went down to see him and wept over him. "My father! My father!" he cried. "The chariots and horsemen of Israel!"*
>
> *15 Elisha said, "Get a bow and some arrows," and he did so. 16 "Take the bow in*

your hands," he said to the king of Israel.

When he had taken it, Elisha put his hands on the king's hands.

17 "Open the east window," he said, and he opened it. "Shoot!" Elisha said, and he shot. "The Lord 's arrow of victory, the arrow of victory over Aram!" Elisha declared. "You will completely destroy the Arameans at Aphek."

18 Then he said, "Take the arrows," and the king took them. Elisha told him, "Strike the ground." He struck it three times and stopped. 19 The man of God was angry with him and said, "You should have struck the ground five or six times; then you would have defeated Aram and completely destroyed it. But now you will defeat it only three times."

20 Elisha died and was buried.

Now Moabite raiders used to enter the country every spring. 21 Once while some Israelites were burying a man, suddenly they saw a band of raiders; so they threw the man's body into Elisha's tomb. When the body touched Elisha's bones, the man came to life and stood up on his feet.

Here life comes from the bones of a dead prophet, and victory comes from the words of an old man. If you are alive and reading these words, then know this: With God, it's not too late to set things straight.

Restored purpose

I remember praying for a young man who didn't have any legs. They were cut off because of an accident. He loosened his pants legs and wanted me to pray for his legs, feet, and toes to grow out. Now I have seen many miraculous healings and I believe God can and fully desires to heal people, but I had a feeling this young man wasn't going to get healed. Then an idea popped into my head as I was praying for him. I asked him how often people walk up and ask him what happened. He told me a few times a week. I said without trying to discourage his faith, "God is desiring to use this tragedy and turn it into a triumphant testimony of God's love in spite of major trials." I exhorted him to try and witness to everyone who comes up to him and asks him what happened. Just think of how many souls would be added to the kingdom if he obeys the word, and how God would be glorified in the midst of a tragic situation.

CHAPTER 3:

Building families, churches and nations

Don't lie to me!

Have you ever given up hope?

Sometimes we can want something so bad, and wait for it so long, that, in the end, it seems less painful to just give up hope. *Forget it,* we say to ourselves. *It just isn't going to happen. Let's get on with life.*

In the prophet Elisha's time, one couple had completely given up hope of ever having children. To even imagine having a son was painful, because they were convinced that all hope was lost. Here's the story from 2 Kings 4:8-17:

> *8 One day Elisha went to Shunem. And a well-to-do woman was there, who urged him to stay for a meal. So whenever he came by, he stopped there to eat. 9 She said to her husband, "I know that this man who often comes our way is a holy man of God. 10 Let's make a small room on the roof and put in it a bed and a table, a chair and a lamp for him. Then he can stay there whenever he comes to us."*

11 One day when Elisha came, he went up to his room and lay down there. 12 He said to his servant Gehazi, "Call the Shunammite." So he called her, and she stood before him. 13 Elisha said to him, "Tell her, 'You have gone to all this trouble for us. Now what can be done for you? Can we speak on your behalf to the king or the commander of the army?' "

She replied, "I have a home among my own people."

14 "What can be done for her?" Elisha asked.

Gehazi said, "Well, she has no son and her husband is old."

15 Then Elisha said, "Call her." So he called her, and she stood in the doorway. 16 "About this time next year," Elisha said, "you will hold a son in your arms."

"No, my lord," she objected. "Don't mislead your servant, O man of God!"

17 But the woman became pregnant, and the next year about that same time she gave birth to a son, just as Elisha had told her.

The Shunammite woman had given up hope. Because she had, Elisha's prediction seemed impossible. It seemed to her that the prophet was lying, that he was playing some cruel joke on her.

Sometimes God will give you a word for someone who has lost all hope. And they may have trouble receiving it, because they cannot imagine the goodness of God stored up for them.

The blessing of children

There is no ache like the ache of a childless couple longing to have children. Throughout history, God has shown His concern and granted children to families who cried out to Him. Scriptures tell us that God "settles the barren woman in her home as a happy mother of children.[76]" From Sarah to Rebekah, from Hannah to Elizabeth, God has granted children to His people when they cried out to Him.

Sometimes, as in this case, the blessing is tied to something the parents did. In Sarah's case, the birth of Isaac was tied to Abraham's faith. In Hannah's case, the birth of Samuel was tied to Hannah's dedication of Samuel to the Lord. And in this case, the Lord blessed this Shunammite couple because they took care of His prophet, Elisha.

Many people are in the world today because of the prophetic. I've seen dozens of people who wanted children. For example, I prayed for one woman who wanted a baby. Six months later when I came back to her church, she was definitely pregnant.

"Look what you did to me!" she said.

I said, "I prayed for you. Be careful what you say."

In one church, I prayed for three couples - and all three conceived children in the same month.

Some prophetic words don't make sense right away. I prayed for a couple in Iowa who couldn't have a baby.

---

[76] Psalm 113:9

The doctor said, "It's impossible." But when many says "impossible," God says, "I'm possible." As I prayed over the husband, I saw two things, an Indian Reservation, and them having a baby. Neither made sense, so they just put those words on the shelf. However, a year later he got a job working for the Boy Scouts, based on what used to be an Indian Reservation. A year after that he called up from the hospital with the news: "We just had a baby!"

In another case, a pastor and his wife had been badly hurt emotionally. As a result, she was closed to having babies. I saw him praying to God to have a baby. When I said that his eyes popped open, but she was filled with fear. God enabled us to break that spirit of fear. We prayed for her. She conceived. Now they have a beautiful baby.

Sometimes adoption is God's plan. I saw one couple either having babies or adopting. They have since adopted two children, and they're very happy.

How can I?

God specializes in doing the impossible. Whether it's children, or finances, or whatever, God delights in showing up and making up for what we lack.

In 2 Kings 4:42-44, God gave Elisha faith to speak God's provision when others could only see the lack.

> *42 A man came from Baal Shalishah, bringing the man of God twenty loaves of barley bread baked from the first ripe grain, along with some heads of new grain. "Give it to the people to eat," Elisha said.*
>
> *43 "How can I set this before a hundred men?" his servant asked.*

But Elisha answered, "Give it to the people to eat. For this is what the Lord says: 'They will eat and have some left over.' " 44 Then he set it before them, and they ate and had some left over, according to the word of the Lord.

A bigger piece of the pie

One lady came up for prayer. As I prayed for her, I thought about the time I visited her home. She and her husband lived in a hundred-year home that couldn't have been worth more than $25,000. I really cared for these people. They were deacons in their church, but they were practically destitute. Their home was a disaster. It was cramped, messy, and uncomfortable.

God gave me a word for her.

"God is going to give you a bigger piece of the pie," I told her.

Her husband doubted, but she said, "I believe that." She had already been coming to a number of our meetings over the years, and she believed in the prophetic.

Six months later I got an e-mail from her husband. He got a job at the Mayo Clinic with a 40% pay raise.

Last Christmas I went to visit them in their new, beautiful, four-bedroom, $200,000 house. It had everything the old house lacked. Everything was new. Everything was clean.

God has totally prospered them.

God is concerned about every area of our lives. God often gives me details about the finances of the person I'm praying for, usually as a way of reassuring them that God knows their situation and is concerned about their finances. For example, God will tell me the amount of someone's house payment, how much a house is worth, how much a car is worth, etc. One time I saw "ten million dollars" over a man. That relates to almost nobody I know. I wondered what he was going to say, but he said, "Yeah, I'm building a ten million dollar building." Then I saw "Catholic church." Again, I knew he wasn't Catholic. But he said, "Correct! I'm buying the land from the Catholic church." I saw several other details; every one was completely related. God saw his situation, and these words were a big encouragement to him and helped confirm his business decision.

For two or three years one man in Madison, Wisconsin tried without success to sell his home. One evening I prayed for him that God would help him sell his home. When he went home from church, he found a message on his answering machine from an interested buyer. He called the buyer back at 9:30-10:00pm. They closed the deal that night.

These are dynamic examples of where God provided. For every story I share, I've seen hundreds of other examples of God providing for His people.

Outside the box

Sometimes God works outside the box.

Bowing before idols is wrong. Yet when Naaman asks for permission to return to the pagan temple, Elisha tells him to go in peace[77]. As a rule, priests were supposed

---

[77] 2 Kings 5:18-19

to marry virgins[78]. Yet God told Hosea to marry a prostitute[79]. Sometimes, what God says doesn't make sense at first.

I prayed over a man who had just gotten saved. I told him, "I see you really prospering. You will serve God, and you will really prosper."

As a result, the young man's faith was built up. But, even though he really believed that word, he didn't know how to prosper. He didn't know how to make money. So, the night after he received the prophecy, he went to the casino. He gambled and won $50,000.

The next weekend he went to church and said to the pastor, "I believe I need to tithe on this, because I want to serve God." He gave the pastor an offering check.

The pastor called me up and asked me what to do.

I said, "Cash it in!"

Please understand that I don't advocate gambling. There are many good reasons never to gamble. But here was a situation where God was able to work outside the box with someone who was brand new in his faith.

Making iron float

Have you ever felt like you were taking one step forward and two steps back? The company of the prophets in Elisha's day experienced that kind of a setback when they tried to build a new place to meet. They started to build, ran into trouble, and needed God's help.

1 The company of the prophets said

---

[78] Leviticus 21:7, 13
[79] Hosea 1:2

to Elisha, "Look, the place where we meet with you is too small for us. 2 Let us go to the Jordan, where each of us can get a pole; and let us build a place there for us to live."

And he said, "Go."

3 Then one of them said, "Won't you please come with your servants?"

"I will," Elisha replied. 4 And he went with them.

They went to the Jordan and began to cut down trees. 5 As one of them was cutting down a tree, the iron axhead fell into the water. "Oh, my lord," he cried out, "it was borrowed!"

6 The man of God asked, "Where did it fall?" When he showed him the place, Elisha cut a stick and threw it there, and made the iron float. 7 "Lift it out," he said. Then the man reached out his hand and took it. [80]

Discouragement will come. Opposition will come. Difficulty is part of life. But God turns tragedies into triumphs.

I prophesied this over one man: "I see the IRS coming against your business. They are going to try to destroy you, but the Lord is going to be with you. You are going to come out of it very blessed."

Sure enough, within the year he was audited by the IRS. The IRS seemed determined to find mistakes and

---

[80] 2 Kings 6:1-7

collect more money. But just the opposite happened. Not only did he not have to pay any money, but the IRS did something it rarely does. When the audit was over, they sent him a check!

Cowbells and church building

Christ builds His church. That involves church buildings, but it involves much more. It means raising up new leaders and new ministries. Many prophetic words have to do with calling people into the ministry. When the prophets in the early church worshipped and fasted, the Holy Spirit spoke to them and said, "Set apart for me Barnabas and Saul for the work to which I have called them[81]."

Through the prophetic, God gives all kinds of ideas on church growth -- ideas on church building, visitation, greeting and so on. I told one Wisconsin pastor, "I saw you putting in a big playland." Since his church is renting a building, this would need to be down the road.

He replied, "Yeah, I have a semi-truck with a playland inside. As soon as we get a building, we'll get it up."

People are working in the nursery, teaching Sunday School, setting up Bible schools, making ministry changes, taking missions trips all over the world -- all as a result of the prophetic.

In 1996, when God first began to use me in a prophetic ministry, I prayed over a man and saw cowbells. I wasn't sure at first what that meant. I later learned that

---

[81]   Acts 13:1-2

the lead cow wore a bell so the other cows would hear the bell and follow.

As I prayed more, the Lord revealed that He was calling this man to be a pastor. This was strange, because, at the time, this man was a member of the Worldwide Church of God, which at that time was a cult! But he gave his life to the Lord, and, over a period of 3-4 years, got filled with the Holy Spirit, attended Rhema Bible College, graduated, and started a church in Rochester, Minnesota. Now his church has about 80 people.

Giving the world a message from the Lord

When Elijah fled from Jezebel, the Lord met with him and predicted that Hazael would be anointed king of Aram[82]. Years later[83], Elisha fulfilled this prediction[84]. Aram was Israel's rival, and the two nations were often at war. But God sent the prophet Elisha to Aram to institute new leadership.

Elisha stepped out of his comfort zone and made the trip to Damascus. In the same way, sometimes we need to step out of the comfort of our churches, and bring a word from the Lord to our world. God gives people words not just for Christians, but for unbelievers. Jeremiah, Ezekiel and other prophets had words over nations, such as Moab, Ammon, Egypt and so on[85]. Isaiah had words over King Cyrus[86]. Much of the prophetic is for unbelievers. 1 Corinthians 14:24-25 tells us that when unbelievers hear

---

[82] 1 Kings 19:15
[83] See "Timing" in Chapter 8 for an explanation of the delay.
[84] 2 Kings 8:7-15
[85] See, e.g., Jeremiah 46 through 51 and Ezekiel 25 through 32.
[86] Isaiah 45

prophecies, that the thoughts of their hearts will be revealed and they will fall down and say, "God is really among you."

We need to believe God for opportunities in the workplace to have a word. God wants to use blue-collar prophets to speak into their companies, to speak a prophetic word over their bosses, to get words over their products, to give direction, to get prophetic words over their co-workers, to have prophetic words over government people.

Paul gave a prophetic word to the soldiers and sailors who were transporting him to Rome[87]. He warned them to wait before setting out on their voyage. Regrettably, they disregarded his prophecy, lost their ship and nearly lost their lives.

In the same way, I've had words over business people who weren't even saved. "Here's what you need to do," I've told them.

I believe in these last days unbelievers are going to seek out Christian prophets to get words of direction in their life. I believe a day is coming when businesses will hire prophets to help increase their profits.

I've had words over nonbelievers who have come to meetings and God has given them clear direction. For example, we had some Mormons come to meetings several times. The first word I got over them was "false religion."

I looked at the guy and said, "I see the word 'false religion,' does that make sense to you?"

He said, "No."

Then I said, "Well, beware of false religions. By the way, what church do you go to?"

He said, "Latter Day Saints."

---

[87]   Acts 27:10

"Okay." Now, obviously, if I were to hammer him at that time, he wouldn't be open.

And so, I've given words about his business that have come to pass. I've given words about his family that have come to pass. Every year they come to our meeting. One time I had a prophecy about them moving. It came to pass.

They've invited me to stay at their home. And the husband said, "I've been trying to get you into the Mormon church to preach. They don't believe the way you do. But, believe it or not, our faith is stronger just because of your ministry."

The wife told me, "We want to get you into the Mormon church."

I answered, "Now that would be God."

Prophesying over the President

When God wants to call new leadership, He often delivers the message through a prophet. Samuel was sent to Bethlehem to anoint David, son of Jesse to replace Saul as king of Israel[88]. God used Ahijah to deliver His calling to Jeroboam[89]. And Elisha instructed an unnamed prophet to anoint Jehu, son of Nimshi, to reign in the place of the house of Ahab[90].

God may give you words of leadership when you are praying over someone else. You may be praying for a three-year-old child and get a word about leadership. But, just as David was anointed king of Israel many years before

---

[88] 1 Samuel 16
[89] 1 Kings 11:29-39
[90] 2 Kings 9:1-13

he finally became king, so also God can bring these words to pass even if it takes a long time.

Here's the story of someone who spoke a prophetic word over the President of the United States.

Lloyd had been a businessman at one time, but he got involved in drugs and alcohol and lost everything. He ended up in Teen Challenge where he came to know the Lord. I met him soon after. At the time of our meeting, he had serious doubts about the prophetic. So he went away by himself and prayed, "God, if this is real, I have three questions." Then he came to me. I prayed for him, and the first three things I said answered his three questions. That's how he came to believe in the prophetic. The Lord gave him other words through me which also specifically came to pass. For example, I saw him in full-time ministry. Within a year he was in full-time ministry.

I saw him about a year later. He said to me, "There's one thing you prayed for me that hasn't come to pass, and it's really bothering me."

"What was that?" I asked.

He said, "You said I was going to have a big ministry and I don't have one yet."

Of course, I thought, *you've been saved one year. Give it some time. I've been in ministry for 20-plus years and I still don't have a big ministry. Come on, give it time.*

Before I could say anything, though, he told me this story.

"In the fall of 2000, just before the November election, I drove a limousine for George W. Bush. While I was driving him, the Lord gave me a prophetic word for him. I told him not to worry about Al Gore. 'You're going to win the election,' I said."

And I looked at him and said, "What! You're trying to tell me that you're wondering when God is going to give you a big ministry? You just ministered to the most powerful man on the planet! Who do you expect to minister to next? Michael the Archangel?"

CHAPTER 4:
How it works

Captain Crunch

One family I prayed for had never been to church. They were Christians, but they were isolationists -- they had never been to church. Someone invited them to a prophetic meeting. They were apprehensive about coming to church in the first place, and even more iffy about the prophetic. They questioned whether the prophetic was even real.

I began by praying over the father. I saw the word "construction." He was in construction. But he looked like a construction guy. Perhaps they thought I could figure that out on my own.

Then I prayed over the mother, and I saw a word that was really hard to share. But the key to the prophetic is sharing what God gives you, even if it doesn't make sense. I saw "Captain Crunch cereal." So I said, "Ma'am, I see 'Captain Crunch cereal.' I know that probably seems really dumb, and I don't know what that means."

I expected her to roll her eyes and think I was being completely frivolous. But, instead, she went hysterical. "We never eat sugar cereal," she said, "But, for my daughter's birthday, the other day, she asked for a box of Captain Crunch cereal."

There's no way I could ever guess Captain Crunch. To me, at first, it seemed stupid. But they knew this word was from God. In fact, they have come back to our meetings, because of Captain Crunch. To you and me, Captain Crunch may mean nothing. But to them it was a message from God.

Sometimes, the Lord will give words that seem unimportant to us, but to the person with whom we are sharing, they are important. God wants to share details about people's lives, so they know God is real, and that He is watching us.

In this chapter, we'll discuss how you can get a message from God to share with others.

Words, pictures and the tickertape

In 1996, I worked briefly with Harold Eatmon, an internationally known prophet from Minnesota. During that time, he explained to me how the prophetic works. He compared the prophetic to a tickertape[91]. "All you do," he said, "is shut your eyes and read the words you see."

I thought to myself, *if reading words is all I have to do, then maybe God will use me. After all, I can read.*

The Old Testament prophet Zechariah clarifies the two main ways in which the prophetic works:

> 7 On the twenty-fourth day of the eleventh month, the month of Shebat, in the second year of Darius, the <u>word</u> of the Lord came to the prophet Zechariah son of Berekiah, the son of Iddo. 8 During the night I had a <u>vision</u> -- and there before me

---

[91] Similar to the words flowing across the bottom of the screen on CNN or ESPN.

was a man riding a red horse! He was standing among the myrtle trees in a ravine. Behind him were red, brown and white horses[92].

Sometimes the Lord will give you a word. Sometimes the Lord will give you a picture.

The Scriptures describe two of the major spiritual gifts as a "word" of knowledge and a "word" of wisdom[93]. Often God will plant a single word in your mind, and your job is to simply speak it out. At that moment, God will either give you the interpretation or another word will begin to form in your mind. I have found, however, that God will usually only give you one word at a time, and it's good He does. Who could remember a whole paragraph?

A little girl came up to me and said, "Why do you shut your eyes? How can you see things with your eyes shut?" It was the cutest little comment. But, if you want to be used of God in the prophetic, you need to learn to get your own thoughts out of the way and shut your eyes and see into the Spirit realm. Another word for "prophet" in Scripture is "seer." The natural man sees things on the outside instead of inside. The way to see on the inside is to shut your eyes and concentrate on Jesus. Then ask God to direct your thoughts. The Bible says "lean not on your own understanding,"[94] You need to pray, "God, give me a word. I'm going to shut my mind off. I need a word for someone."

Sometimes, God will give you pictures. In this

---

[92] Zechariah 1:7-8 (emphasis added)
[93] 1 Corinthians 12:8
[94] Proverbs 3:5

case, and it's like watching a video. All you have to do is describe what's happening. This can be fascinating. I have been able to see minute details such as the cereal someone eats, the color and type of the car he drives, the dog he owns, the type of job he has.

I prayed over a man in Florida. I saw that he had a call to minister in his life. As I started sharing with him about the call, I found out he wasn't a believer. He was a backslider. The word didn't seem to fit. So I led him back to Christ. He gave his life back to the Lord, but the prophetic word about a call to the ministry still seemed out of place. As he was about to leave, I saw a picture of a black Lexus.

"I see a black Lexus," I said. "Does that mean anything to you?"

"Yes, it does. I own a black Lexus!"

In this case, this picture from the Lord was like a deposit guaranteeing the call of God in his life. If God could show me the make and color of the car he drove, then it was truly God who spoke the word about this man's calling.

After this revelation, the man admitted that, yes, God had called him to the ministry when he was a young man, but he ran from the calling. When I saw the black Lexus, it all came together.

Here's how the prophetic typically works through me: After the church service, people come forward for prayer. I pray for them one at a time. I shut my eyes, and, as I begin to pray for each person, I will see words or pictures. I may see words such as "Caterpillar," "abortion," "rejection," "racism." Or I may see pictures, such as a filling station, a person riding a motorcycle, someone eating breakfast. Then I share with the person what I see. If, at that point, I don't have a clear interpretation I will ask the person if that word or picture means anything to them. If it hits home (and it does about 98% of the time) I will pray for them.

Sometimes words don't make sense right away. Sometimes the person is fearful or for some other reason they can't understand what's happening. In those cases, I may ask a friend, a relative or the pastor if they understand the word or picture. If they don't have any understanding I will pray and like pieces of a puzzle it usually all comes together, and by the end of the prayer time we have an understanding of what God is saying.

Occasionally, however, nobody understands what it means and then I encourage the person to pray about it and if nothing comes to their mind just shelve it. I prayed for one lady and saw "swings." But nobody had a clear understanding of what it meant. She was irritated and even called the pastor to complain. A week later she applied for a job. Halfway through the interview she asked what the company was all about. The answer: "We make swings." Bingo!

When the word doesn't make sense right away, you may be tempted to try to force a meaning or an interpretation. Don't do it! This can cause untold troubles and we place ourselves in danger by adding to what God is saying. It's okay to say, "I don't know what this means, but lets put it on the shelf."

Pray and intercede!

If you make yourself available to pray for people, and you shut off your mind and begin to pray in the Spirit,

God will begin to drop words or pictures in your mind that will touch the person you are praying for. The prophet Samuel understood the importance of intercessory prayer[95]. To him, failing to pray for Israel was a sin.

For me personally, the prophetic anointing seems the strongest during times of praying for others. Sometimes people are praying for me and without knowing it they are prophesying in the midst of their intercession. If you want to move in the blue-collar prophetic anointing you must make it your goal to stay in an attitude of prayer. I love what the great healing evangelist Smith Wigglesworth said: "I never pray longer than fifteen minutes, but I never go more than fifteen minutes without praying."

Hearing the voice of God

The prophets I'm acquainted with see words as opposed to hearing them. I have never heard of anyone who hears the words out loud. And only twice have I heard God's voice audibly. But, when I did, God used that audible voice in a powerful way.

Here's one of those incidents: I was ministering in a church in South Dakota. An older woman came forward, and she in a crisis point in her life. She was very nervous about what she should do. Should she sell her property or not? I heard someone say "Century 21." And I was telling her, "I see you selling some property, why don't you look up Century 21?" Then I said, "By the way, who said that, who said, 'Century 21'?" But no one had said it. I heard God's voice out loud. It was exactly right, because we needed an accurate word from God for her.

---

[95]   1 Samuel 7:5,8; 12:23

Asking questions

Sometimes I get a question or I turn the word into a question. Jesus often asked questions. I may get a question like, "Has someone rejected you?" Of course, everyone has been rejected at some time. But, the point is, that might be the most important thing in their life right now. Or I may see a word such as "finances." Instead of saying, "I see the word 'finances,'" I may ask, "How are your finances going?"

"We can't pay the bills."

In a case like this, we need to believe God for something. We don't just need a word of knowledge, but a word of wisdom to know what to do about those finances. Or we need a gift of faith to believe God for a miracle.

A picture can be worth a thousand words.

Almost half the time, I see pictures. For example, a man came forward, I prayed for him and saw a red car. He had just purchased a red car. And he knew that there was no way I could have known that.

The first time I got a picture from the Lord, I saw the man I was praying for riding a Harley, going the wrong way, and ending up in an accident. This was the first time I had ever been in that particular church, and I had only been flowing in the prophetic for two months. Nobody knew that he had just bought a Harley the day before and that he had stopped at a bar that night. He had almost walked in and decided not to. Instead, he came to church. When I saw him on a Harley going the wrong way, it stirred him that he was going in the wrong direction. It was the perfect word picture. It let him know that God was watching.

I have also seen pictures of people being attacked,

or in sin. Or doing positive things. Many times I see pictures of someone cooking food, giving something away or doing some kind act, and being unappreciated. She thinks nobody cares. Her work is unnoticed by the world, but it's noticed by God. These kinds of pictures are powerful. When I share them, I often see tears in people's eyes as they begin to realize, *I'm not a nobody. I'm a somebody. God saw what I did.*

Rudolph the Red-Nosed Reindeer

One junior high girl came up for prayer. I saw a picture of Rudolph the Red-Nosed Reindeer. Not exactly a very spiritual word. She was wrestling with some concerns about her appearance, and I said, "I bet you feel like Rudolph the Red-Nosed Reindeer."

She later told me that before the meeting she was outside, it was cold, and her nose was red. She told the girl who invited her, "Look, I look like Rudolph the Red-Nosed Reindeer." She even had a Rudolph the Red-Nosed Reindeer necklace on that I couldn't see.

God used an image to reassure her that He was watching over her.

Other ways in which the prophetic works

Scripture not only describes the prophetic as coming through words[96] and pictures or visions,[97] but also through dreams,[98] burdens,[99] and a burning fire within.[100] A friend

---

[96] Jeremiah 2:1, Amos 1:1, etc.
[97] Isaiah 1:1, Amos 8:1, etc.
[98] Daniel 2:17 etc.
[99] Nahum 1:1, Habakkuk 1:1 etc.

of mine in Seattle gets one dream after another. His dreams make sense. His dreams come to pass. Once in a while I experience a prophetic dream, but not often. Some people have visions. These visions go beyond simply seeing a picture or a video. In these cases, it's like you are there. Sometimes, when I pray for people, a burden will come over me, a burden for salvation, or for marriage or family problems. A burden is a heaviness of heart. Sometimes you can just feel it -- a spirit of heaviness, of depression. Often I will get a burden like this when the person I'm praying for is suicidal.

Sometimes you may get a burning fire inside. Jeremiah tried to stop prophesying, but he could not because there was a "fire in his bones."[101] There will be words you just have to speak out. Sometimes when I'm praying the fire of God will burn in me, and I prophesy in power and anointing. In those cases, people are lit up with the glory of God and the power of God. You may have a fire that burns in your spirit. When you speak it out by faith, you will discover it is transforming.

For example, in Iowa I prayed over a long-haired man in his fifties. I saw the word "preacher." But there was a yoke of bondage on him. When I began to preach at him, God broke the power of that yoke and he started screaming and shouting. Six months later, I spoke with his son who is also in the ministry. He said, "My dad is on fire. He's preaching. He's sharing Jesus with people." The

---

[100] Jeremiah 20:9
[101] Jeremiah 20:9

anointing broke the yoke, but it was a fire that came from my bones. This burning is a powerful thing that happens in your spirit.

Sometimes the prophetic flows through the presbytery. Several prophetic people will be gathered together to prophesy. One person will have a word. Then another. Then another. It just flows from one person to another person to another person. That is also a powerful way that God speaks through people.

During counseling sessions, God will give me words for people. In prophetic counseling, the prophet gets a word from God and shares it before he asks the person to share their problems.

Remember the story of Nebuchadnezzar. On pain of death, he required his advisors to not only tell him the meaning of his dream, but also to tell him the content of the dream.[102] In one sense, Nebuchadnezzar's reasoning was correct: If God can show us what the dream is, then He certainly can provide a valid interpretation. Likewise, if God can show the problem, then He can also show the solution. Anybody can give counsel, but how do you know if your counsel is God's counsel?

The prophetic has three parts: (1) the word, (2) the interpretation -- what it means, (3) application -- wht to do with the word. Getting words is relatively easy. The tough part is interpreting and applying the word. Here's where people make mistakes.

---

[102] Daniel 2:1-49

"I see a snake around your neck."

I saw a snake around one lady's neck. But I wasn't sure what it meant. So I said, "I see a snake around your neck. Go home and destroy it."

She cooked up her own creative interpretation. She went home and told her husband, "The prophet says I have a snake around my neck, and I need to destroy it. You're the snake. I have a boyfriend. I'm going to drop you and go after him."

Well, duh! Anybody who's got a brain would know what the correct interpretation was. But she didn't know.

Naturally, her husband was upset. He came to church the next evening. He came looking for bear and I was the bear. He told me the story, and he was hot.

I said, "You're not the snake. The boyfriend is the snake."

That cooled him down. He liked that interpretation. He told his wife, and she got rid of the boyfriend. And I like that interpretation too, because I'm still alive.

Even prophets and apostles in the Bible had trouble with interpretations and applications.

You can have the right word and wrong interpretation. As the apostle Paul was traveling, he was met by a prophet named Agabus. Agabus took Paul's belt, bound his own hands and feet, and predicted that Paul likewise would be bound by the Jews in Jerusalem and handed over to the Gentiles.[103] Everyone present thought this was a warning not to go to Jerusalem, and they begged Paul to reconsider his plans. But Paul knew there was a

---

[103] Acts 21:10-14

difference between a word of knowledge and a word of wisdom. The prediction of Agabus was accurate, but he didn't understand that Paul's arrest and imprisonment was all part of God's plan.

Agabus had a right on word, but he didn't know what to do with the word.

When Jesus reinstated Peter, Jesus predicted Peter's crucifixion. Peter wondered what would happen to John. Jesus answered, "If I want him to remain alive until I return, what is that to you?"[104]

Many people interpreted that word to mean that John would live until Jesus returned. But that, of course, was the wrong interpretation.

Before Jesus ascended into heaven, the apostles were expecting him to fulfill Old Testament prophecies by setting up a political rule right then and there. But they were wrong.[105] So, if the apostles made mistakes, we're all going to make mistakes.

Prophecy can be tricky. Think about it. How many contrary teachings are there about the book of Revelation? If that's true with the written word, what about personal prophecy?

Getting the right interpretation

When I pray for people, I usually allow people to interpret the word I have over them. I might say, "What does this mean to you?" I might say, "I see 'anger.' What does that mean to you? Do you have an anger problem? Did your parents have an anger problem? Do your kids

---

[104] John 21:22
[105] Acts 1:6-7

have an anger problem? What does that mean to you?"

Unlike the lady with the snake around her neck, normally, a person is more apt to be able to interpret their life. I usually give him or her the option of interpreting that word.

Be careful about forcing interpretations and applications. Scripture admonishes us not to add or subtract from God's Word. Sometimes you'll get a word and the interpretation will come later. In those cases, you need to let the word rest and see what happens. When I saw the word "amputee" over the stroke victim,[106] I could have tried to force an interpretation. But, by letting it rest, God was able to bring a far more powerful interpretation to that stroke victim, a life-changing interpretation.

Some words have double meanings. Isaiah predicted that the virgin (or young woman) would conceive.[107] The prophecy had a double fulfillment, once in Isaiah's time,[108] and once in the birth of Jesus.[109] I might get a prophetic word for someone, and it might also relate to the person who is standing right next to them also. Some words will relate to two or three people or a whole church.

Anointing to break the yoke

It's not enough just to have the right word or the right prophecy. You need the anointing to break the yoke. There are yokes on people that prevent them from fulfilling

---

[106]   see Chapter 2
[107]   Isaiah 7:14
[108]   Isaiah 8:3
[109]   Matthew 1:18-23

their prophecies. Your goal is not just to speak the correct word -- Caiaphas has a correct word -- Balaam had a correct word -- but you need the anointing to break the yoke. And that comes from a relationship with Jesus.

Word pictures - God's surgical tool

When David committed adultery with Bathsheba, God could have sent Nathan to David with the message, "You have committed adultery and murder." But He didn't. Instead, He had Nathan share a word picture.[110] When Nathan told David the story about the rich man who stole the poor man's only sheep, he evoked a powerful emotional response in David. Only then was David able to see the enormity of the sin he had committed.

When we sin, a hardness forms in our hearts toward God. But God can use a word picture to navigate around that hardness to the place where our hearts are still soft.

People try to protect themselves. Sometimes God will give indirect words to get around their self-protection. They need to drop their guard for God to deal with them. This happens especially with very painful events, where people have blacked them out, or blocked them out, and do not want to discuss them. God will give an indirect word and, all of a sudden, boom, I can see it in their eyes. God connects with the root issue and brings deliverance.

God often uses these kind of images and symbolic language to convey messages. He showed Amos, a farmer,[111] a basket of ripe fruit.[112] The point had nothing to

---

[110] 2 Samuel 12:1-14
[111] Amos 7:14

do with fruit. Rather, God was showing the prophet that the time was ripe for judgment. The book of Revelation is filled with symbolism. Sometimes symbolism allows God to deliver a message with a time-delayed interpretation. Sometimes the interpretation won't make sense until the prophecy is fulfilled.[113] I prayed over a 65-year-old woman and saw a baby. Unless she's Sarah, she's not going to birth any babies. But the image had a symbolic meaning, i.e., that her dreams would come to pass. I saw someone getting stretched. Obviously, he wasn't going to grow from 5'4" to 6'3", but instead he would be stretched spiritually.

Living word pictures

God sometimes uses creative ways to communicate his message through prophets. Not only does He have prophets give messages orally[114] and in writing[115] but also sometimes the prophet's life was a living word picture.[116] An example of a living word pictures is Hosea who married a prostitute. When she ran away, he loved her and brought her back. His wife, Gomer, was a living word picture of backslidden Israel.[117]

God cares about privacy.

Families have family secrets. Sometimes they are evil. Evil secrets need to be brought out and dealt with.

---

[112] Amos 8:1-2
[113] Although not symbolic, the word in Psalm 69:9 finally made sense when fulfilled in John 2:14-17.
[114] e.g., 2 Kings 1:16-17
[115] e.g., Jeremiah 29:1-23
[116] e.g., Ezekiel.12:3-6
[117] Hosea 1:2-3, 3:1-3, etc.

But sometimes they are not evil. There are some things you just don't share. For example, maybe a child has a bedwetting problem. You don't share that with everybody. God likes to keep things in the family. He protects our privacy.

That is why God will sometimes share words using symbolic language. He loves His child and he doesn't want His child to be ashamed or embarrassed. God doesn't want to ruin people. He wants to heal people.

I may pray over someone about a very sensitive issue that doesn't make sense to everybody listening, but it makes a whole lot of sense to the person I'm praying for. I may get symbolic words or images, and have no idea what they mean, but the person I'm praying for will say, "I know what it means." And I say, "Good." The purpose is not for me to understand, the purpose is not for the messenger to always understand, the purpose is for the one receiving the message to understand. That way some of the things are kept private, so nobody else knows. But the person knows, and he or she is glad nobody else knows.

We prophesy in part.

As a blue-collar prophet, you are only responsible to share those things the Lord shares with you. If He doesn't share anything with you, you aren't obligated to share a message He hasn't given you.

Some things will be hidden from you. When the son of the Shunammite woman suddenly died during harvest, the woman hurried to find the prophet Elisha. In 2 Kings 4:27 we read:

When she reached the man of God at
the mountain, she took hold of his feet.

Gehazi came over to push her away, but the man of God said, "Leave her alone! She is in bitter distress, but the Lord has hidden it from me and has not told me why."

God reveals what we need to know in order to do His will more perfectly at one particular time and place. A prophecy is only one small insight into God's will for our lives. Even Moses didn't get everything all at once.[118]

Because we prophesy in part, prophecy unfolds progressively in our lives. Take Abraham, for example. At about age 50, he was told to leave Ur.[119] He and his father and their family settled in Haran. But God told him to leave Haran.[120] In Canaan, God revealed that He would give this land to Abraham.[121] He gives further details about this inheritance later.[122] At his wife's urging, Abraham tries to realize the fulfillment of the prophecy that he would have a son, by taking Hagar as a concubine.[123] But God reveals a better plan years later,[124] and Isaac was born.[125]

God will give you a word. The scripture talks about *a word* of knowledge or *a word* of wisdom. God may not give a whole sentence or a paragraph. God doesn't tell every detail about a person's life. If He did it would be more like fortune telling, I believe.

---

[118] Compare Exodus 3:1-4:17 with Exodus 4:24
[119] Acts 7:3
[120] Genesis 12:1-5
[121] Genesis 12:7
[122] Genesis 13:14-17
[123] Genesis 16:1-16
[124] Genesis 18:1-15
[125] Genesis 21:1-7

We prophesy in part because God wants His people dependent on Him, not on His prophets. He expects His children to read their Bibles, to pray, to hear the voice of God,[126] to go to church, to listen to a spouse, and to seek out godly counsel. The prophetic is only one way to hear from God. We don't want Christians needing to consult a prophet for every personal decision they make.

My advice for people is this: Don't go to a person to get a word. Go to God to get a word, and He may use a person.

The prophetic puzzle

The prophetic is like a puzzle. Imagine your life as a 10,000 piece puzzle. And during the time of the prophetic, God may only give you five pieces. Sometimes the pieces fit right together, and they make sense.

But, just like a jigsaw puzzle, some pieces don't seem to fit anywhere at first. They don't seem to fit right until the whole puzzle is finished. When the puzzle is finished, you look and say, "Oh, that's where that piece fits."

I prayed over a couple in South Dakota about having a baby. And I saw a picture of the sun. They didn't know what the picture of the sun meant and I didn't know. Their desire was to adopt a baby. They had been waiting for years to adopt a baby. They had to remain constantly available because the adoption agency could call them at any time telling them a baby was ready for them to pick up. In fact, over the course of a year, the agency called them seven times, and seven times they went to the hospital only

---

[126]   Romans 8:18

to find out that the birth mother had changed her mind. They were so frustrated that they were ready to quit the church. At that point, the lady finally admitted that she was making children her idol. She repented, and they decided to take a break and visit some friends in Phoenix. They set the adoption goal to the side, and booked a flight for late January 2002.

Meanwhile, in mid-January I came back to their church. While I was preaching a series of meetings at their church, they got another call from the adoption agency. They picked up their baby and two days later flew to sunny Phoenix.[127]

"Sunny" didn't seem to fit with "baby" at first. But, in the end, God brought the pieces of the puzzle together.

Foretelling vs. forth-telling

Prophecy is about predicting the future, right?

Not necessarily. A high percentage of prophecy has to do with the past and the present.

We are a product of past decisions and experiences -- both good and bad. Because God is Alpha and Omega, the Beginning and the End, he can bring healing to past wounds and hurts that affect us to this day. I have found over and over again that we are bound by past decisions, relationships, experiences and mistakes. As the Holy Spirit reveals these chains, we are released from the past and are able to go forward and become all that God has for us.

For example, David opened the door to the devil by having an affair with Bathsheba. When Nathan the prophet came and gave him a prophetic word picture and concluded

---

[127] Even the basketball team is called the Phoenix Suns.

by saying, "Thou are the man!" David was grief-stricken and repented before the Lord God. In this case prophetic forth-telling revealed the past, dealt with the present, and enabled David to go forward with God in the future.

Sometimes a past word can boost faith for a future word. Saul's family lost their donkeys. Saul went to consult Samuel, but before he could even bring up the issue of the lost donkeys, the prophet assured him that the donkeys had been found. Samuel gave Saul past words to enable him to believe God's prediction that Saul would be king of Israel.[128] If God can give you a word for where you've been and where you're at right now, it's easier to believe a word for where you're going. God knows your past, so He also knows your future. I have found, in my experience, that God will reveal the past to gain credibility to give you a word for the future. Many prophetic words are hard to believe, but when God reveals something from the person's past or present, it is easier to believe that kind of word. Hundreds of times I have shared details about a person's life that are undeniable such as their name, relative's name, occupation, prayers they pray, personality traits, sports they like, etc. This "now" word becomes a springboard to encourage them to believe the foretelling (future) word that may be difficult to believe and achieve.

Another purpose of revealing the past is so much of the foretelling (future) prophetic is based on "if-then" conditions, meaning, if you obey, then God will come through. Coaches and teachers know that humans need immediate incentives to keep us going. In a similar manner, God wants to give us prophetic words that offer hope so we

---

[128]   1 Samuel 9 especially verse 20

are motivated to change.. That is why He gives us words that require us to walk in total obedience in order for them to be fulfilled.

Prophecy is tied to other gifts

The Bible mentions nine manifestation gifts in 1 Corinthians 12:8-10: (1) word of wisdom (2) word of knowledge (3) faith (4) healing (5) miracles (6) prophecy (7) discerning of spirits (8) tongues (9) interpretation of tongues. Prophecy works in concert with these gifts. God may give you discerning of spirits, for example, to recognize counterfeit gifts.[129] Sometimes, when I'm praying for people and nothing comes to mind, I begin to pray in tongues and then words or pictures will come. Sometimes when I have a difficult or delicate word to share, a corrective word or a potentially embarrassing word, praying in the Spirit helps me know how best to share this difficult message. Also, after praying for hours it's easy to become weary, so when you pray in the Spirit, it gives your mind a breather to be built up and strengthened in the Holy Ghost. God will use a prophetic word to show which part of a person's body he wants to heal. The Lord may give a powerful word that is difficult to believe in the natural, but then he will give the gift of faith to believe it.

---

[129] Matthew 24:24

CHAPTER 5:
Getting started

How I got started

Over 60,000 times the Lord has spoken a prophetic word through me. But there was a time when I had no idea how to move in the prophetic. I didn't learn it in Bible college. Even though I attended a Pentecostal college for four years, no one told me how the prophetic worked. In fact, I didn't learn how to move in the prophetic until years later, when I was working with an anointed prophet named Harold Eatmon. In the process of working with him, I learned how the prophetic worked, and his prophetic mantle fell upon me. Up until this time, I had been going from church to church conducting evangelism seminars, giving the same twelve sermons over and over again. But a pastor friend said to me, "I see you preaching sermons -- new ones." Then he laid hands on me and imparted the prophetic anointing. The next week I was prophesying over people. Three weeks after that a revival started in Sioux City, Iowa and my whole ministry changed.

God wants to speak through you. This chapter will show you how to get started in a blue-collar prophetic ministry.

Get wisdom

"I do not want you to be ignorant."[130]

These words of the apostle Paul reflect God's desire for you to understand spiritual gifts and how God wants them to work in your life. Many believers either do not see that we have a need for Spiritual gifts or they have never taken the time to find out what the Word of God has to say about them. The fact is the entire Bible is a prophetic word from the Bridegroom to his bride. The Bridegroom wants us to understand the gifts He has lovingly provided for us. The Scriptures command us to study diligently to show ourselves approved unto God, a workman that won't be blushed with embarrassment.[131] Sadly, many Spirit-filled believers have little or no understanding of what God has to say about the prophetic anointing.

The Bible is the place to start. But you can also gain a great deal of wisdom by reading books by well-respected authors such as Rick Joyner, Bill Hamon, Kenneth Hagin and Mike Bickle that give the ABCs of moving in the prophetic. I would encourage you to hang around a prophetic ministry and watch carefully how God uses them. Stephen and Phillip were just table waiters, but as they hung around the men of God something must have rubbed off for these two men were used mightily by the Holy Ghost. In the Old Testament, people could go to learn the prophetic in the school of the prophets. In modern times, there are schools of ministry designed to train prophetic ministers.

Stephen is described in the book of Acts as a man of

---

[130] 1 Corinthians 12:1
[131] 2 Timothy 2:15 paraphrased

wisdom. When you begin to learn new ideas and put them into practice, God Himself will begin to teach you unique things to help you personally flow in the prophetic. Normally, we need to be faithful and learn from others before God gives us divine insight on a more personal basis. I have found that I can learn bits and pieces from other prophetic men and women that I can put into practice into my life. If you truly desire to flow in the prophetic, why not travel with a prophetic person for a week or two and "carry their bags" and learn from them? Soon you will begin to see words, visions and pictures in the Spirit realm in a clearer fashion than you do right now.

You gotta want it!

How did Elisha get his prophetic anointing? Look at this passage from 2 Kings 2:

*1 When the Lord was about to take Elijah up to heaven in a whirlwind, Elijah and Elisha were on their way from Gilgal. 2 Elijah said to Elisha, "**Stay here**; the Lord has sent me to Bethel."*

*But Elisha said, "As surely as the Lord lives and as you live, **I will not leave you**." So they went down to Bethel.*

3 The company of the prophets at Bethel came out to Elisha and asked, "Do you know that the Lord is going to take your master from you today?"

"Yes, I know," Elisha replied, "but. do not speak of it."

*4 Then Elijah said to him, "**Stay***

**here**, Elisha; the Lord has sent me to Jericho."

And he replied, "As surely as the Lord lives and as you live, **I will not leave you.**" So they went to Jericho.

5 The company of the prophets at Jericho went up to Elisha and asked him, "Do you know that the Lord is going to take your master from you today?"

"Yes, I know," he replied, "but do not speak of it."

6 Then Elijah said to him, "**Stay here**; the Lord has sent me to the Jordan."

And he replied, "As surely as the Lord lives and as you live, **I will not leave you.**" So the two of them walked on.

7 Fifty men of the company of the prophets went and stood at a distance, facing the place where Elijah and Elisha had stopped at the Jordan. 8 Elijah took his cloak, rolled it up and struck the water with it. The water divided to the right and to the left, and the two of them crossed over on dry ground.

9 When they had crossed, Elijah said to Elisha, "Tell me, **what can I do for you** before I am taken from you?"

"**Let me inherit a double portion** of your spirit," Elisha replied.

10 "You have asked a difficult thing," Elijah said, "yet if you see me when I am taken from you, it will be yours- otherwise not."

11 As they were walking along and talking together, suddenly a chariot of fire and horses of fire appeared and separated the two of them, and Elijah went up to heaven in a whirlwind. 12 Elisha saw this and cried out, "My father! My father! The chariots and horsemen of Israel!" And Elisha saw him no more. Then he took hold of his own clothes and tore them apart.

13 He picked up the cloak that had fallen from Elijah and went back and stood on the bank of the Jordan. 14 Then he took the cloak that had fallen from him and struck the water with it. "Where now is the Lord , the God of Elijah?" he asked. When he struck the water, it divided to the right and to the left, and he crossed over.

15 The company of the prophets from Jericho, who were watching, said, "The spirit of Elijah is resting on Elisha." And they went to meet him and bowed to the ground before him.

[emphasis added]

Elisha knew what he wanted and he didn't give up until he got it. Look at the results:

God used Elijah to raise the dead once.[132] God used Elisha to raise the dead twice.[133] Elijah brought rain.[134]

---

[132] 1 Kings 17:17-24
[133] 2 Kings 4:18-37, 2 Kings 13:20-21
[134] 1 Kings 18:41-45

Elisha healed a spring[135] and brought water in the desert.[136] Elijah fed a widow and her son.[137] Elisha fed a hundred men.[138] Elijah prayed and fire fell from heaven.[139] Elisha trapped a whole army,[140] lifted a siege,[141] brought victory to armies.[142] God used Elijah to confront.[143] God used Elisha to heal,[144] to curse,[145] to restore,[146] to anoint,[147] to deliver,[148] and to decontaminate.[149] Elijah brought judgment.[150] Elisha did too,[151] but he also restored hope.[152]

To get the double portion Elisha had to:

- ☐ Keep walking until he got it.
- ☐ Keep talking with those who had it.
- ☐ Keep watching. He developed perception, discernment, and sensitivity by watching and copying Elijah.

He was persistent. He was tenacious. He hungered

---

[135] 2 Kings 2:19-22
[136] 2 Kings 3:1-27
[137] 1 Kings 17:7-16
[138] 2 Kings 4:42-44
[139] 1 Kings 18:16-40, 2 Kings 1:9-15
[140] 2 Kings 6:8-23
[141] 2 Kings 6:24-7:20
[142] 2 Kings 3:1-27, 13:14-19
[143] 1 Kings 17:1, 21:17-28, 2 Kings 1:16-17
[144] 2 Kings 5:1-19
[145] 2 Kings 2:23-24, 5:20-27
[146] 2 Kings 6:1-7, 8:1-6
[147] 2 Kings 8:7-15, 9:1-13
[148] 2 Kings 4:1-7
[149] 2 Kings 4:38-41
[150] 1 Kings 18:40
[151] 2 Kings 2:23-24, 5:20-27
[152] 2 Kings 4:8-37

for the things of the Spirit. And he asked for hard things. The Bible says to "eagerly desire spiritual gifts, especially the gift of prophecy."[153]

How bad do you want the gifts? God can use anybody. If you want them bad enough, you will have them.

You gotta want it.

Ask for it

Do you want to move in the prophetic?

Ask. Ask God. God says,

Call to me and I will answer you and tell you great and unsearchable things you do not know.[154]

"Call" in this verse means to call out to someone, to cry out, to address someone, to shout, to call out loudly.[155] Sometimes it means to name something or call it by name like God did when he called the day and night into being.[156] The word "unsearchable" means isolated or inaccessible.

So pray. God is not stingy. He will not withhold good gifts from you.[157] God wants to get His message across. He has used donkeys,[158] false prophets[159] and even the man who condemned Jesus to death.[160] He wants to use

---

[153] 1 Corinthians 14:1
[154] Jeremiah 33:3
[155] See Isaiah 55:6; Joel 2:32
[156] Genesis 1:5
[157] Matthew 7:11
[158] Numbers 22:28-30
[159] See Numbers 22-24, 31:16, 31:8, Joshua 13:22, Jude 11, Revelation 2:14
[160] John 11:49

you.

Ask God for His gifts. Don't quit.[161] Ask and keep on asking.[162] Knock and keep on knocking. Knocking is an aggressive action. Knocking says, "Open the door, man, I want some anointing." I want the gifts. I know one man who used to come to our meetings just to please his wife. He was the last one there and the first one to leave. At first he had a sour attitude. But as time went on, he started moving from the back to the middle to the front. After a year or so, he was coming early to pray with me. Now he has a prophetic ministry in his church.

Don't neglect to read the Word of God. Stand in God's council.[163] If you want to move in the prophetic, you have to know God. John, the author of Revelation, had the greatest prophecies in the New Testament. More New Testament prophecy was written by John than anyone else, more than everyone else put together. Why? John had a revelation of Jesus. John spent time with Jesus. John laid his head on Jesus' chest. Don't sacrifice intimacy with God.

And understand what you are asking for. These are gifts from God. The gifts give people a lift. The gifts heal people. The gifts set people free. The gifts inspire people to love God and other people more.

Hopefully, you will ask with good motives. Hopefully, you will ask in order to have a better ability to share the love of God with your generation.

But let me make a bold statement. I think it's

---

[161] Galatians 6:9
[162] Luke 18:1-8, Matthew 7:7-11
[163] See Jeremiah 23:21-22

selfish to not want to be used in the gifts of the Spirit. To not want the gifts is more self-centered than to want the gift for poor reasons. God is more than able to change our inadequacies or our fleshly desires. Paul talked about people who preach out of wrong ambitions, but he rejoiced that at least the gospel was preached. In a similar fashion, people who are used by God may have all kinds of faults, but they are being used by God to help others.

Seek the Giver AND the gifts

Some people say, "I am seeking God's face, not his hand." I prayed recently for a man who said, I don't ask God for things. I don't believe I should ask God for things.

I'm sorry, but that's contrary to Scripture. The Bible says, "Ask and you shall receive,"[164] "Call unto me,"[165] "Let your requests be made known to God,"[166] and "You have not because you ask not."[167] We shouldn't think God doesn't want to be bothered. "Bother Me!" He says. "See what I can do for you."

There is a balance here. On one hand, resist the temptation to only seek God for signs and wonders while neglecting an intimate relationship with Him.

But don't throw the baby out with the bath water.

The Scriptures command us to: *"...eagerly desire the greater gifts..."*[168] and *"Follow the way of love and eagerly desire spiritual gifts, especially the gift of prophecy*

---

[164] Matthew 7:7
[165] Jeremiah 33:3
[166] Philippians 4:6
[167] James 4:2
[168] 1 Corinthians 12:31

."[169]   God chooses strong language here; He wants us to eagerly desire, to covet, to long for. God rewards those who earnestly seek Him.[170]

Are you seeking God for the prophetic anointing? If not, why not?

On the other hand, don't neglect to seek God's face. Seek the Giver AND the gifts. Covet spiritual gifts. But seek God. Remember the warning of Jesus:

> *"Not everyone who says to me, 'Lord, Lord,' will enter the kingdom of heaven, but only he who does the will of my Father who is in heaven. Many will say to me on that day, 'Lord, Lord, did we not prophesy in your name, and in your name drive out demons and perform many miracles?' Then I will tell them plainly, 'I never knew you. Away from me, you evildoers!'"[171]*

There is a very real danger here. A relationship with God will stimulate prophecy. But, just because God uses you doesn't mean you have a relationship with God. Balaam had true prophecies, even though he was a false prophet.[172]   Caiaphas gave a true prophecy, but he

---

[169]   1 Corinthians 14:1
[170]   Hebrews 11:6
[171]   Matthew 7:21-23
[172]   See Numbers 22-24, 31:16, 31:8, Joshua 13:22, Jude 11, Revelation 2:14

murdered the Lord Jesus.[173] So true prophecy doesn't mean you have a true relationship with God.

Remember, Gehazi was being groomed to be the next Elisha. But Gehazi had a spirit of coveteousness on him. He sought gain and lost everything.[174] Just because God uses you, don't lose your caution. Just as greed destroyed Gehazi, so also pride can destroy you. Be careful. This is why we devote an entire chapter to the importance of holiness in the life of the blue-collar prophet.

Stir up the gifts

Paul gave this instruction to Timothy: *"Therefore I remind you to stir up the gift of God which is in you through the laying on of my hands."*[175] "Stir up" means to stoke up the fire. When God fills us with the Holy Spirit then all of his omnipotent power, anointing and gifts are in us. Because of ignorance or lack of interest we can let our fire go out. That's why God commands us to stoke up our spiritual fervor.

How do you stoke the fire?

Prayer stirs up the gifts of the Spirit. Many people don't pray fervently. But the Bible says, "The effectual fervent prayer of a righteous man availeth much."[176] The context of this passage talks about healing. If you want to bring healing, pray fervently.

The church will stir up the gifts of the spirit. You will see the prophetic flow when there's a fiery worship

---

[173] John 11:49, 18:13-14,24,28
[174] 2 Kings 5:27
[175] 2 Timothy 1:6
[176] James 5:16b KJV

service. Music stirs up the prophetic.[177] Worship stirs up the gifts of the Spirit. Get rid of garbage music, and start tuning into the Spirit and see what God does.

Anointed people stir up the gifts. Hang around the anointing. I know a couple who drive to every revival they can find. They serve as deacons in their church. They are committed first to their local church. But they go to all these meetings. As a result, they are flowing in the Spirit.

You need faith

You need to prophesy by faith, because God may have a message for someone that makes no sense to you. One time I was praying for the unsaved husband of a Christian woman. He was Hispanic. The Lord gave me the word "puente." I had no idea what "puente" meant, but I spoke it out by faith. They explained to me that "puente" means bridge. Then I knew the interpretation. Jesus Christ is the Bridge to God. I explained this. The man's eyes lit up, and he prayed to receive Christ. For him, receiving a Spanish word that I didn't understand was a sign from God. No wonder the Scriptures say, "If a man's gift is prophesying, let him use it in proportion to his faith."[178]

Prophesy doesn't come from your own good works. Like salvation, it is a gift from God. It is not earned or deserved.[179] We're not filled by the Spirit because of our good works. We're filled with the Spirit because God loves us. It's a gift and He wants His children to have it. God doesn't give you prophecy because *you're* a really good

---

[177] See, for example, 2 Kings 3:15

[178] Romans 12:6

[179] Compare Ephesians 2:8-9 with Romans 12:6 and Galatians 3:5

person. He gives you prophecy because *He's* a really good God.

Prophecy comes from faith. You must believe, first of all, that God is going to speak to you. And, when He does, you need to exercise faith to speak out what He tells you. Of the 60,000+ prophecies I've given, only twice did I hear the audible Word of God. The rest is all by faith.[180] You will prophesy, then, according to the amount of faith that God has given you. Some people have less faith. Their words are more general, but that's where their faith is. The exciting this is this: Our faith can grow.

When I first started out, my words were general, like "broken heart," "rejection," "finances," or "marriage problems" -- things that most people can relate to. As my faith grew, the words became more specific. Now God gives me names of people, zip codes, cereal choices. One time I got the word "Mutambo." I wondered if it might refer to the Denver basketball player. But when I spoke it out, the person I was praying for told me that it meant "gift" in his mother tongue.

God will give you a mustard seed of faith. Exercise it, and your faith will grow.

How do you build your faith?

"Faith comes by hearing, and hearing by the Word of God."[181] Pour yourself into the Word of God. Study it. Memorize it. Meditate on it. Speak it aloud. And your faith will grow. Just as God breathed on the writers of

---

[180] See Chapter 4
[181] Romans 10:17 KJV

Scripture,[182] so also, God will breathe on you to speak His word.

Most of the Bible is written by prophets. As you read the word you begin to realize that God does want to speak to people. God spoke to nations. He wants to speak to you and through you.

Hang around the anointing.

The second way to get faith is to hang around the anointing. This is so important. Hang around people who are anointed. The Spirit of prophecy will begin to move mightily, and people who hang around anointed people will begin to get prophetic words.

People have traveled with me, or just walked up and stood nearby when I was praying for people, and they've begun prophesying. One lady who was part of a denomination that doesn't typically move in the prophetic, prophesies right along with me on numerous occasions. Another time, my brother-in-law was with me when I was praying for someone in New Mexico. I saw a cowboy boot, and I also saw this sharp thing on the back of the cowboy boot, the thing that spins. For the life of me, I could not remember what that was. I could not think of the name. Of course, I know now. But, at the time, my mind went blank. As I was struggling to remember the word, my brother-in-law was standing next to me thinking, *if he asks me what I see, I'm going to tell him I see a "spur."* Finally, I said, "I see a spur." He about fainted. The spirit of prophecy was so obvious. God was trying to speak.

When two or more people get together to prophesy

---

[182]   See 2 Peter 1:19-21

over someone, this is called a presbytery. One person gets a word. Someone else gets an interpretation. Another person gets an application. As I have trained churches in the prophetic, I am amazed at the accuracy and anointing these new "trainees" have. It seems as if the Spirit flows more powerfully in a group than in one person.

In God's kingdom the way up is the way down. Many people want the power gifts, but they're not willing to serve God in minor things. We can't ignore the Scripture to not despise small beginnings.[183] By serving we learn and grow. Nobody starts at the top. We go through a period of preparation. Serve in your local church. Serve a prophetic ministry. Moses spent forty years in the wilderness watching sheep.[184] Paul spent three years in the desert and then years serving in the church in Antioch before he got started in his ministry.[185] Stephen who received more coverage in Acts than most of the apostles, started by serving at tables.[186] Elisha poured water on Elijah's hands[187] for ten years, before his anointing was imparted.[188] Elisha was being groomed. How do you get groomed? You hang out with the anointing. You see how it works. You watch how it works. You learn. The more you learn, the more confident you feel. You start seeing the same things in the Spirit that your mentor sees.

Mentors are important. Elijah mentored Elisha. Moses mentored Joshua. Paul mentored Timothy. Even

---

[183] See Zechariah 4:10
[184] Acts 7:30
[185] Galatians 1:17, Acts 11:25-30; 12:25-13:3, 13:9
[186] Acts 6:1-6
[187] 2 Kings 3:11
[188] 2 Kings 2:1-15

David started out as an armor bearer for Saul.[189] The great evangelist D.L. Moody impacted Billy Sunday, who in turn, impacted Mordecai Hamm, a former professional boxer. When Hamm went to preach in Georgia, he got kicked out of town. So he preached outside of town, and Billy Graham got saved. Anointing goes from generation to generation.

Pursue the anointing. You are not necessarily pursuing the man, it's pursuing the gift in the man you want. The man may have his problems. But the gift in the man -- that is what you need.

Anointing is more caught than taught. Simon the Sorcerer became a Christian, but when he saw the power of God, he tried to buy it. He couldn't do it,[190] and neither can you. You cannot buy the anointing. You cannot get it by going to seminary. But you can get it by serving those who have the anointing.

In 1996, I served a prophet named Harold Eatmon, and his prophetic mantle fell on me.[191] Jesus said, "He who receives you receives me, and he who receives me receives the one who sent me. Anyone who receives a prophet because he is a prophet will receive a prophet's reward, and anyone who receives a righteous man because he is a righteous man will receive a righteous man's reward."[192]

Some prophetic ministries operate a school of the prophets where you can get apprenticeship training in the

---

[189] 1 Samuel 16:21
[190] Acts 8:18-24
[191] See Chapter 4
[192] Matthew 10:40-41

prophetic. We have started such a school. I am training people how to move in the prophetic. I teach for a short time, and then, as a group, we practice prophesying. Then we divide up in small groups and I oversee what God is doing. It is a great experience. And the prophets judge. Other prophetic ministries operate similar schools. If you are interested in something like this, give us a call at 1-800-785-6695. I'd be happy to talk to you about training opportunities.

Fight fear with faith

One word can change the course of a person's life. A career change. A sin issue. A marriage problem. Raising a child. I prayed for a 13-year old girl who hadn't seen her dad since she was a baby. I said, "I believe God is going to have him call." The next night he called, and they got together. Prophecy is powerful.

The gifts of the Spirit are powerful. They are life changing. The devil does NOT want you to use them. There is a spirit of fear attached to the gifts of the Spirit. Not by God, but by the devil.

Fear stops the prophetic. Many people, because of fear fail to share what God wants them to share. But we need to let the gifts of the Spirit flow through us, uninhibited by fear. Share the word when God gives it to you. It may not make sense, and it may not seem to fit, but share it by faith, and trust God to bring it to pass. God has not given us a spirit of fear, but of power, love and a sound mind.[193] Jesus said, "I am telling you now before it happens, so that when it does happen you will believe that I

---

[193]   2 Timothy 1:6-7

am He."[194]   Share it now.   Don't wait until a prophecy unfolds and tell someone, "Oh, I knew that."   Prophecy is saying it before it happens.   That way, God gets the glory.

Oops! What about mistakes?

I prayed for a couple in Seattle. We were praying in the back of the church. The lights were off in the back part of the church because they were preparing for worship up front. I thought I was praying for this woman and her husband. But the man I was praying for was not her husband. He was another guy. As I laid hands on him, my mind was attached to her husband. As a result, I prophesied accurately according to her husband, but not according to the person I was praying for.

She finally let me know, "This is not my husband."

Oh! This makes sense.

What did I do? I didn't say, "Thus saith God, I'm right." I just said, "Oh, I made a mistake. I was prophesying over your husband. Not over the person who was here."

I make mistakes. You will too. Everybody does. Nobody is 100%. I'm not infallible. Neither are you. Admit your mistakes, or you will lose your credibility. I've had to call people and say, "I've made a mistake." I've had people come up, and I can't even tell if I'm talking to a guy or a girl. I've asked God, "Is this a guy or a girl?" And I don't know which they are. I can't tell. I ask for a name.

Answer: "Chris."

Okay, "What's your middle name?"

---

[194]   John 13:19

104

"Pat."
Wonderful!

Making mistakes doesn't stop me from prophesying. Many times I get words that make no sense to me, and I wonder if I'm making a mistake. But I speak them out anyway, then 99% of the time, the word makes sense, if not initially, then later. As the recipient meditates on the word, God shows him or her the meaning. It is in the waiting period where faith comes in.

Everybody makes mistakes
The fact of the matter is - Nobody is 100%. If everybody was 100%, then the Bible wouldn't say, "Let the prophets judge." It says, "Let two or three prophets judge." If there was 100% accuracy, then God wouldn't say, "Let the prophets judge."

Many people will turn to Deuteronomy 18:20-22, and claim that true prophets won't make mistakes. Usually this is a way of arguing that there are no true prophets because everybody does make mistakes. Here's the passage:

> *20 But a prophet who presumes to speak in my name anything I have not commanded him to say, or a prophet who speaks in the name of other gods, must be put to death."*
> *21 You may say to yourselves, "How can we know when a message has not been spoken by the Lord ?" 22 If what a prophet proclaims in the name of the Lord does not*

take place or come true, that is a message the Lord has not spoken. That prophet has spoken presumptuously. Do not be afraid of him.

But this passage must be considered within the context of the whole Bible as well as human experience. How do you learn to ride a bike? By falling down. How do you learn to prophesy? By trying, and sometimes making mistakes. In the Old Testament, there was an prophetic apprenticeship program,[195] and there appeared to be an organized school of the prophets.[196] Joel predicted that young and old, men and women will prophesy.[197] If prophecy is open to all,[198] then obviously some are going to be new at it. Some will be learning. Some will make mistakes.

In the Old Testament, there were career prophets whose job was to hear from God. Old Testament prophets heard God's voice audibly. There was no questioning whether the word was from God. In the New Testament, we have to discern God's voice. We must listen carefully to His sweet voice. Sometimes, we make the mistake of speaking from our own spirit and not the Holy Spirit. In the Old Testament, the prophets needed courage to speak the prophetic word that they heard audibly. In the New Testament, we need courage to speak out what we feel, sense or discern that God is quietly speaking in our heart.

---

[195]   2 Kings 3:11
[196]   E.g., 2 Kings 9:1
[197]   Joel 2:28-29
[198]   1 Corinthians 14:1, 29

In the New Testament, we "prophesy in part,"[199] and the prophets must judge.[200] The passage doesn't say that the mistake-maker must be stoned. It merely says that the prophets must judge whether the word is accurate.

Because we make mistakes, I recommend you back away from statements like, "Thus saith the Lord." Instead, say, "This is what I see," "This is what I believe the Lord is saying," and "Does this make sense to you?"

You will make mistakes. Don't be afraid of that. If you do, admit them, and move on. As I read Mike Bickle's book, *Growing in the Prophetic*[201] (which I believe is must reading for those interested in the prophetic), he states that most of their prophets will see a word or vision and then ask the recipient what they think the word or vision means. Their ministry in Kansas City is one of the chief training grounds for the prophetic in the United States. But even the "best of the best" don't know it all. God alone is omniscient.

Laying on of hands

A pastor laid hands on me and imparted the prophetic anointing. The next week I was prophesying over people. Three weeks after that a revival started in Sioux City, Iowa and my whole ministry changed.

Jesus compares the flow of the Spirit to rivers of living water.[202] Sometimes the rivers get plugged up. By the laying on of hands you release the river. And it begins

---

[199] 1 Corinthians 13:9
[200] 1 Corinthians 14:29
[201] Mike Bickel with Michael Sullivant, *Growing in the Prophetic*, Charisma House, 1996.
[202] John 7:37-38

to flow.

Spiritual gifts are often imparted by the laying on of hands.[203] One of the anointings of a prophet is to raise up people to move in the prophetic. Many times I'll pray over people and I'll see the prophetic anointing falling upon them. As I declare that the prophetic unction is preparing to fall on them, they reply, "I've been praying about that!" So my word comes as confirmation.

Who should lay hands on you? Someone with clean hands. If the person's hands are dirty, don't let them lay hands on you. I don't let people I don't know lay hands on me. I may not want what they have. If I don't know where their hands have been, I don't want them on me.

The gift of prophecy may be imparted through lay people. As a rule, however, it is best to have proven prophets lay hands on you because they can impart a prophetic anointing. I also believe that your pastor should be in agreement. Pastors know character traits and other information that keeps prophets from laying hands on someone prematurely.[204] Prophets know things in the spirit realm, but some things they don't know. Some things are hidden from them.[205] Samuel was 0 for 7 when he went to anoint David.[206] Samuel kept thinking that one of David's brothers would be king. Eventually, Samuel got it right.

You may have to pursue the impartation of this spiritual gift.

---

[203] Romans 1:11, 1 Timothy 4:14
[204] 1 Timothy 5:22
[205] E.g., 2 Kings 4:27
[206] 1 Samuel 16:6-11

Elijah tried to dodge Elisha.[207] But Elisha said, "Hey, where you go, I go. I want that anointing, man!" Elisha was a pest, in a sense. Some are called to be pastors. Most of us are called to be pesters. There are people who dog me. They keep hanging around. One guy calls me up, "I'll watch your book table, I'll help you with your newsletter, anything! I just want your anointing." And he's getting it. He sees visions. He sees accurate prophetic words.

Do you know what? I don't mind if he bothers me. You gotta want it. Do you want it?

---

[207] 2 Kings 2:2,4,6

CHAPTER 6:
Holiness: the life of the blue-collar prophet

Repenting before the service

I lost my temper one night. But just before the church service, I hurried up and repented because I wanted God to use me. And God did use me. I gave one prophetic word after another that was right on. But it was probably the most miserable service I've ever been in. I struggled the whole way through. Afterward, the Lord said to me, *Tom, don't ever do that again.*

God doesn't just want the Holy Spirit to flow through you. He wants you to be holy.

Two sides to the same coin

The gifts don't come by good works. But God does expect you to be pure. The Holy Spirit is called the *Holy* Spirit because he wants you to be holy.

What's on a penny?

"Abraham Lincoln," you might say.

And I might answer, "No, it's the Lincoln Memorial."

Is it Abraham Lincoln or is it the Lincoln Memorial?

Well, both are inscribed on a penny. Both are

equally right.

It's the same way with the gift of prophecy. On one hand, the sovereign Lord can use anybody He wants in the prophetic. On the other hand, He wants you to be holy.

Faith activates the gift of God. But holiness makes the use of the gift pleasing to God.

God commanded the Israelites to bring pure oil of pressed olives for the lamps in the tabernacle.[208] The prophetic is like a lamp. It goes into the shadows of men's hearts. It goes into the shadow of God's plan, and reveals things that are hidden. But God wants us to be a vessel of honor, an article for noble purposes.[209]

As a blue-collar prophet, part of your job is to expose sin. I have seen everything from adultery to homosexuality to abuse. Christ desires to use you to purify His bride, the church. How can He do that if you aren't walking in purity yourself?

Just as a highway patrolman tends to slow down traffic, so also a strong prophetic ministry in a church tends to produce righteous living.

When I was a student in Bible School, Rev. Ernie Moen shared a message with us that I will never forget. "There are three things," he told us, "that a minister needs to stay away from: the gold, the glory, and the girls[210]." If you are not prepared to distance yourself from sin, even flee from sin, you have no business moving in the prophetic.

---

[208] Leviticus 24:2
[209] 2 Timothy 2:20-21
[210] Obviously, he spoke to a male audience. The point is to avoid inappropriate relationships of any kind.

The trap of greed

Before I began moving in a prophetic ministry, I traveled for nine years teaching churches how to evangelize. During that time, I often made the comment, "If you want to make money in the ministry, then you need to move in signs and wonders." This can be so true. Sometimes, a lot of money can flow into a prophetic ministry. That's why blue-collar prophets must take care not to run after the kingdom of thingdom. You can't be in it for the money.

Greed was Balaam's error. He wanted to obey God, but he wanted to make money. The elders of Moab and Midian tried to hire Balaam to give them the prophecy they wanted: a curse on Israel. Because Balaam's heart was divided by his greed, his prophetic anointing was prostituted for the prospect of financial reward.[211]

To get an idea of how God feels about the greed that corrupts those who should be the messengers of God, consider this passage in Jude:

> *11Woe to them! They have taken the way of Cain; they have rushed for profit into Balaam's error; they have been destroyed in Korah's rebellion. 12These men are blemishes at your love feasts, eating with you without the slightest qualm--shepherds who feed only themselves. They are clouds without rain, blown along by the wind; autumn trees, without fruit and uprooted--*

---

[211] See Numbers 22:7, 22:32, 31:16, Deuteronomy 23:4-5, 2 Peter 2:15, Jude 11

twice dead. 13They are wild waves of the sea, foaming up their shame; wandering stars, for whom blackest darkness has been reserved forever. [212]

A pastor in New Mexico gave me this compliment: "I knew Tom was legitimate, because he prayed for all of the poor folks first." Of course, I didn't know who was poor and who was wealthy, but I do know how much people give for our monthly support. It is tempting to prophesy good things to people who give the most money. It is also tempting to pray for the big givers first and leave the children and poor until the end. But we cannot do that. We must fear the Lord and trust Him to guide us. James warns us to never treat rich people better than poor people. Favoritism, James declares, is directly at odds with the "royal law" of loving your neighbor as yourself.[213]

Here are some guidelines I have used since 1986. If you are a traveling minister, you might consider adopting something similar:

1 Let pastors take up your offering.

2 Never use a prophetic word to manipulate money from another believer.

3 Personally, I rarely teach on giving, I feel that's the job of the pastor of the local body.

4 Remember, God is not poor, and He is the one who signs your paycheck.

5 Don't try to get people to feel sorry for you, so

---

[212] Jude 11-13
[213] James 2:1-8

they will give more.

6 Be a giver yourself. Sometimes traveling ministries seem greedy. We must set the example on how to give.

There are times I pray over people and I say, I see you traveling with me. It's not really for my benefit. It's for their benefit. And that's okay.

But prophesying for your own benefit is wrong. For example, if I prophesy to someone, "Give me your car," or if I say, "I see five people here who should give me a thousand dollars," that's manipulation, and control, and -- as far as I'm concerned -- it's witchcraft. Prophesying for gain, or control or manipulation is a form of witchcraft.[214]

Gehazi lost it all.

The Lord healed Naaman of leprosy through the prophet Elisha.[215] When Naaman saw that he was healed he offered Elisha a gift.[216] This was no small token of thanks. His gift included 750 pounds of silver, 150 pounds of gold.[217] It was like winning the lottery.[218] Elisha would have been set for life. He would have had incredible wealth to do anything he wanted to do. Imagine what he could have done with his ministry. Think of the prophetic schools he could have started. And perhaps he could have used his wealth to buy influence to counteract the worship of Baal and all the other false religion in the land.

---

[214] See, e.g., Ezekiel 13 esp. v. 19, also 22:28, 1 Samuel 15:22-23
[215] 2 Kings 5:1-14
[216] 2 Kings 5:15
[217] 2 Kings 5:5
[218] 2 Kings 5:26

Naaman's offer must have been incredibly enticing.

But Elisha turned it down flat. "No way," he said. Even when Naaman urged him to accept, Elisha refused.[219] Then Elisha was able to deal with a more important matter: Naaman's relationship with the true God, the God of Israel. Naaman set off to return to his own country, having been healed and finding peace with God.

But Gehazi, Elisha's servant, fell into the trap of greed and self-serving nationalism. Here's the story from 2 Kings 5:

> *19(b) After Naaman had traveled some distance, 20 Gehazi, the servant of Elisha the man of God, said to himself, "My master was too easy on Naaman, this Aramean, by not accepting from him what he brought. As surely as the Lord lives, I will run after him and get something from him."*
>
> *21 So Gehazi hurried after Naaman. When Naaman saw him running toward him, he got down from the chariot to meet him. "Is everything all right?" he asked.*
>
> *22 "Everything is all right," Gehazi answered. "My master sent me to say, 'Two young men from the company of the prophets have just come to me from the hill country of Ephraim. Please give them a talent of silver and two sets of clothing.' "*
>
> *23 "By all means, take two talents,"*

---

[219] 2 Kings 5:16

said Naaman. He urged Gehazi to accept them, and then tied up the two talents of silver in two bags, with two sets of clothing. He gave them to two of his servants, and they carried them ahead of Gehazi. 24 When Gehazi came to the hill, he took the things from the servants and put them away in the house. He sent the men away and they left. 25 Then he went in and stood before his master Elisha.

"Where have you been, Gehazi?" Elisha asked.

"Your servant didn't go anywhere," Gehazi answered.

26 But Elisha said to him, "Was not my spirit with you when the man got down from his chariot to meet you? Is this the time to take money, or to accept clothes, olive groves, vineyards, flocks, herds, or menservants and maidservants? 27 Naaman's leprosy will cling to you and to your descendants forever." Then Gehazi went from Elisha's presence and he was leprous, as white as snow.

Gehazi was being groomed to be Elisha's successor. But he lost everything. Greed blinded Gehazi to the more important issues of God's glory and God's desire to reconcile men to Himself. Greed so twisted Gehazi's mind, that he forgot that God can see hidden sin and that He uses His prophets to expose it.

When Ananias and Sapphira tried to hide their sin from the Lord, Peter was given a word of knowledge that exposed this sin.[220]   What was the result?   *"Great fear seized the whole church and all who heard about these events."[221]*   When there is a genuine fear of the Lord, people will begin to repent and come clean. The Lord Jesus is purifying His bride.

The trap of glory

Pride will stop the prophetic.

Whenever we have a certain amount of success in anything, we have tendency to think that we are extra special which opens the door to pride. I was ministering in a church when a person came up for prayer. I said that I was glad to see them. The visitor responded that he would drive 100 miles, no 1,000 miles, to hear me minister. At that very moment, the Spirit of God rose up in me and said, "Watch out for pride." So I dismissed the compliment and grabbed a hold of the humility that is in Christ.

God resists pride. If you feel like you are a somebody because God used you, watch out! The Lord will not share his glory with anyone else and He will go out of his way to resist you. There is nothing worse than trying to serve a God who is resisting you. We are simply mailmen and all we are doing is delivering the mail. If you don't take the credit when you get a "right-on" word, then you don't have to feel bad if you get a word that doesn't seem to make sense.

Christian ministry is NOT about what *we do* for God. Christian ministry is about what *God does* through us. Maybe that's why God doesn't typically choose the

---

[220]   Acts 5:1-11
[221]   Acts 5:11

richest, the smartest, or the most beautiful.[222]

The pruning process

When I was in Bible College I was blessed to be able to hear awesome men of God like Pastor Cho from South Korea, C.M. Ward, Rich Wilkerson and other great men and women of God. They inspired me. I wanted to be super anointed and used of God. I hate to admit it, but a part of me wanted to be noticed also. "God, use me with signs and wonders," was my prayer, but I was thinking, *then I'll be on TV and everybody will see me.*

Why do you want the gifts? The purpose of the prophetic is not to make you look good. It's not to make you feel good. It's to help other people. Your heart must be right.

God does desire to honor those who honor him. For example, God honored Abraham[223] and David.[224] Yet most of us need to have this area of life sanctified. If you desire to be used of God, get ready to be pruned, steamed, boiled, tested ... need I go any further? By the time God is done with us, all we want to do is glorify his name. When that happens, then if God honors us, fine. And if He doesn't, that's fine too.

Before God pours his gifting on us, the Lord will prune us from self-glory. Bill Hamon says, "God makes the man, before He manifests the ministry." And he adds, "God will not deal with advanced root problems during a productive ministry season. He will bring the minister and

---

[222] 1 Corinthians 1:26-29
[223] Genesis 12:2 etc.
[224] 2 Samuel 7:9 etc.

his or her ministry into a winter season of inactivity and non-productivity. He will plow the prophet upside-down, exposing the root problems, and then he will either spray them with a strong anointing to destroy them or else rake the minister' s soul until all the roots are removed and thrown into the fire of God's purging purpose."[225]

From 1986 to 1995, I traveled and conducted over 500 evangelism seminars all across North America. Then the Lord allowed me to go through a deep pruning process that wiped out most of my self-confidence.

It's interesting, when I was at my lowest is when God was at His highest. When I had lost everything in my life, the anointing came.

I owned a million dollar business and I lost it all. I was down in the dumps, working a job I hated. I lost everything in my life. When I finally hit bottom, God said, "Go back in the ministry."

"God," I cried, "I have nothing to offer." I had finally reached the bottom of Tom Stamman. By the time the Lord was done with me, I realized that without God's power I couldn't do anything. I was so decreased in my own eyes and everyone else's eyes, that I felt I was nothing. I began to embrace what John the Baptist said, "I must decrease that He may increase."[226]

Then God replied, "Now you are called. Now you are ready."

I was brought so low that I would never feel like I'm better than people.

God's pruning process is ongoing. Bill Hamon

---

[225] Bill Hamon, *Prophets, Pitfalls & Principles*, p. 10
[226] John 3:26-30

adds, "We must allow God and those He has appointed as our spiritual overseers to show us our weed seed attitudes and remove the newly-sprouted character flaws before they grow intertwined with our personality and performance. The longer we wait, the more drastic the process becomes."[227]

In 1999 I went to a revival in Smithton, Missouri to get a refreshing touch from the Lord. I have to admit the meeting was a little out of my comfort zone and I had to resist getting a critical spirit. I was looking forward to receiving a prophetic word. The first man prayed a nice word over me. But I didn't drive eight hours to receive a nice word. I wanted to know what was blocking me from more anointing. The Spirit of God instructed me if I wanted to get corrected, to ask another brother to pray for me. So I walked up to him, and he prayed for me. He started telling me things about my life. I need to change this and change that. Basically, he was spanking me in the Holy Ghost. It was great. There were some changes. I adjusted. God wants to purify his bride. Sometimes we need to let God tear the walls down, so his Spirit can freely flow through us.

God commanded the Israelites to use pure oil from *pressed olives*. How do you get oil from olives? Squeeze them. God will squeeze you. He will squeeze your character. There are times when I've prayed for the rapture. I can't take it anymore. Everybody probably goes through that. But the prophets, particularly, will get squeezed. They will go through very difficult times. Daniel was

---

[227] Bill Hamon, *Prophets, Pitfalls & Principles*, p. 10

thrown in the lions' den.[228]   Shadrach, Meshach and Abednego were thrown into the fiery furnace.[229] Jeremiah was thrown into a cistern.[230]

Our job is to build up, not tear down.

Many people misunderstand the prophetic. They feel that the prophet's job is to be hard on people to get them to change. They imagine themselves denouncing sin and delivering fiery rebukes like Elijah or Jeremiah. They love Old Testament images of prophetic power that rebukes the sins of the nation.

And it is true that one of the jobs of a prophet is to denounce sin. But the New Testament gift of prophecy is primarily designed to comfort, edify and exhort. In fact, the Scriptures tell us not to rebuke an elder.[231]

For example, John's prophetic words in Revelation 2 & 3 contain warnings and admonitions against sin. Yet, these rebukes are sandwiched in between encouraging words, affirming good deeds and promising blessings for repentance.

No one (including prophets) wants to be criticized continually and reminded of their own faults all the time. If you want your child to fail, just harp on his faults all the time and never praise good behavior. If you want him to succeed, remember that we all need positive reinforcement.

When Jesus prophesied Peter's denial,[232] He didn't hammer on him. He didn't quote the scripture, "If you

---

[228] Daniel 6
[229] Daniel 3
[230] Jeremiah 38
[231] 1 Timothy 5:1
[232] Luke 22:31-32

deny me, I'll deny you." Instead, He said, "When you have returned to me, strengthen your brethren." In other words, "Peter, you are going to fall away, but I know that you love me, so when you come back -- and I know you will -- help your brothers." He could have denounced Peter and said, "I see Ichabod over you, the glory of God is departed from you, for you have denied me, and, therefore, unless you repent you will be dropped into the abyss and left there with all of the other non-committed Christians."

Prophecies like this will alienate you from the rest of the body.

There is a time to reprove people. Sometimes God gives me words of correction for the people for whom I'm praying. But the goal of this correction, and of most prophecies, is to encourage people to change, so they can walk in the fullness of the Spirit and the blessings of the covenant.

Suppose your boss said, "You need to work a little faster. If you do, I will give you $5.00 per hour raise." You would probably be motivated to work faster. But suppose your boss said, "You are the laziest person I have ever met, and if you don't pick up the pace I am going to fire you." What would you do then? Chances are you would start looking for a new job.

With these things in mind, I recommend that only mature prophetic ministries that are recognized by other leaders and ministers correct others.

Your private life makes a difference in your public ministry.

I got saved when I was seventeen years old at a Bible camp in Missouri. Four months later I decided that waiting on God for a Christian girlfriend was unrealistic, so

I began to contemplate dating an unbeliever. (If you believe in the fallacy of "missionary" dating, good luck! You will need it, because God won't bless dating an unbeliever.) About that time, I was invited to hear an evangelist named Brian Ruud. This man had a powerful testimony. When he gave the altar call, I decided to recommit my life to Christ. I went forward to meet with the evangelist. He was about 6' 3' with an afro that made him look about 6' 7". He looked down at me and asked if I would give up every thing for a pretty girl. I am a talker and rarely am I at a loss for words, but his question so shocked me that I began to babble. I was so embarrassed that my face turned beet red. I was wearing a bright yellow turtleneck and I looked like a sick tomato. I immediately repented and got right with God. I never forgot this experience, and I never dated an unbeliever again.

Christians are called to a certain standard of purity. Prophets may be called to an even higher standard. God may ask you to avoid gray areas where others can participate. For example, I can't go to health clubs. I love to go to health clubs. I worked in health clubs for five years. I was a member of health clubs for eight years. But I don't go because I don't want to be walking in temptation. And so that's for me. For you, going to health clubs might be okay. But for me, I can't do that. I don't watch anything demonic on TV or movies. I don't want to watch any borderline stuff that has to do with psychics and that sort of thing. If I discover any hint of the demonic or psychic or anything related on a video we own, I throw it away. I don't want anything to do with it.

God wants us to watch our private life. How do you live when no one is watching? Do you look at pornography? Do you allow yourself to dwell on those evil thoughts? What God sees in secret, He rewards openly.[233]

You can't pour water from an empty glass.

As blue-collar prophets, we are constantly being called upon to give words, counsel and prayer. When we lay hands on people, prophesy and pray, we are giving life to others. When the woman with an issue of blood touched Jesus, He said, "power has gone out from me."[234]

To give, we must be filled up. We cannot give from an empty vessel. If a well runs dry, the water tastes bad, then stops flowing altogether. A nursing mother must keep on feeding herself healthy food so that her baby will be healthy. If a mother does not get enough calcium, then the nursing baby will literally take calcium from the bones of the mother.   If a mother continues to neglect herself physically, she and her baby will get sick and weak.

Likewise, blue-collar prophets must continually feed themselves, or they will get weak spiritually and be open to Satanic assaults.

Here are some of the things that I try to do to keep fed. You can tailor your own spiritual workout from these.

☐ Read 7 chapters of the Bible a day (five in the old and two in the new).
☐ Before each service, pray an hour.
☐ Limit times of fellowship during the day before each service.
☐ Avoid television.
☐ Limit recreation.
☐ Study books and listen to tapes of other anointed men

---

[233] Matthew 6:6
[234] Luke 8:46

125

and women of God.

If you want to be led by the Spirit, see into the Spirit, hear from the Spirit, then you should be filled with the Spirit. In Ephesians 5:18 Paul says, "Do not get drunk on wine, which leads to debauchery. Instead, be filled with the Spirit." The phase "be filled" refers to a continual filling. Almost every day I pray, "Lord, fill me with the Spirit." This, I believe, is one of the reasons that the gifts keep on flowing through me. God wants to fill everyone of us so full of His Spirit, that we will look for opportunities to let the Spirit of God flow out of us to bless God's people.

Another key is drawing near to God, so He may draw near to us.[235] How do we do that? We join with Paul in praying that we *may have power, together with all the saints, to grasp how wide and long and high and deep is the love of Christ, and to know this love that surpasses knowledge -- that you may be filled to the measure of all the fullness of God.*[236]

As we begin to grasp how much Jesus loves us, we begin to fall in love with Him. This deep, intense love draws God into our being. This intense longing for the presence of God draws the power of God into our souls so it can be released out of our being in the form of signs and wonders. As we draw near to God, His fullness begins to pour into our lives resulting in a flood of love that is so overwhelming that it spills into the lives of others through the fruit and gifts of the Holy Spirit.

---

[235]   James 4:8

[236]   Ephesians 3:18-19

CHAPTER 7:

Opposition: the price of the anointing

"The world is full of suffering, and it is full of overcoming it."
-- Helen Keller

A word for the devil worshipper

The deacon I was with said, "I think we should witness at the mall."

"Why?" I asked.

"Because I don't want to. I'm afraid," he said.

"What are you afraid of?"

"Teenagers. There are teenagers at the mall."

It seemed strange to me. He had teenagers of his own. But, no problem, we went to the mall. And, sure enough, outside the mall were about a hundred teens.

I started witnessing to six or seven teenagers. Things were going well, until two other guys decided to start a fight. That drew a crowd of about seventy-five kids. And the people I'm witnessing to decided they wanted to watch the fight first and get saved later.

That would never do. There was only one thing to do. Break up the fight.

So I jumped in the middle of these two kids who are about to duke it out.

It was at this moment that God said, *Now's your time to preach.*

Preach! What do I preach about?

But God said, *Don't worry about it.*

So I said, "Hey, everybody. How many here, if you died tonight, know you're going to heaven?"

A couple of teenagers raised their hands.

And I said, "Why?"

People from the crowd shouted out, "I'm good." "I'm bad." "I'm rad." (Sometimes you need the gift of interpretation of tongues to talk to teens.)

I said, "Well, I think you guys might be going to hell." Then I started preaching the gospel. And God was moving.

Then the police arrived and invited me to leave. Since I didn't have any money for bail, I felt led to comply.

As I was walking away, I saw a teen in a car, and I just felt that he needed God. I walked up to him and said, "You need Jesus."

He gave me an answer I didn't expect. He said, "I can't." Not, "I won't," or "Someday I will," but "I can't."

I pursued it. I walked up to him and said, "You need Jesus."

Again he said, "I can't."

Then a girl in the back seat said, "We hate you. We're devil worshippers."

I handed her a tract and said, "You might hate me, but I love you."

She said, "I'm going to rip up this tract."

"No, you won't," I said, "in Jesus' name."

That scared her. She didn't rip it up.

Three months later, we went back to the same mall. We shared Christ with a number of kids. When I was about ready to call it a night, someone said, "Here come the Jesus freaks. Here come the Jesus freaks."

I went over to talk to her, and after a few minutes I recognized her. "Oh, you're the devil worshipper," I said.

She said, "Yes, I am," in a deep, demonic voice.

I saw that her windshield wiper was broken, and I offered to pay someone to fix it. It didn't work out, but, at least, I offered.

Then the Lord gave me a word for her. "You were abandoned by your mother and father," I said.

"Yeah," she answered. "They dropped me on the doorstep of my neighbor's house." She went on to tell the horrifying story of her abusive childhood, of seeing people hung upside down and cut in two for the devil, and of witnessing babies being sacrificed to Satan.

I said, "God loves you. Even though you hate me, and love the devil, I tried to pay someone to fix your windshield wiper because Jesus loves you."

She looked away. But I could see she had tears in her eyes.

She was persecuting us. But she got a word from God. She had a problem and God touched her.

Expect opposition.

If you expect to move in the prophetic and not get any opposition, I'm afraid you're in for a rude awakening. People will oppose you. Jesus said, "Woe to you when all men speak well of you, for that is how their fathers treated the false prophets."[237]

Satan knows what happens when God's people begin to rise up and move in the power of the Holy Spirit. He will begin to put obstacles in your way to prevent you

---

[237] Luke 6:26

from fulfilling your destiny. He wants to keep you from sharing God's plan and purposes with others.

The devil knows that if he can discourage you and dissuade you by sending an obstinate person so that you will quit the call of God on your life, then he will send that person to you. The Bible says, "I shall not be moved."[238] I hang on to that scripture. If you want to walk with the Lord, decide right now that you will not let the devil move you and shake you off the foundation of Jesus Christ.

When the devil saw that he couldn't detour Jesus by tempting Him in the wilderness,[239] he arranged to have him persecuted in his hometown of Nazareth.[240] One minute his fellow Nazarenes were praising him, the next minute they were trying to push him off the edge of a cliff. You can go from glory to gory, and from hero to zero in warp speed if you choose to speak the truth.

Persecution is the price of a good life. Some people don't like us. The devil hates us. We get nasty phone calls. We had a Harley man stop at our home one day. He walked right into our house without knocking. Two of my children ran out of the house. A week later, a detective from Minneapolis informed us that a group called the Outlaws had been looking for us. They got ticked off at us. We've had Satanic people come to our meetings. Sometimes psychics come and try to ruin things. We've had people rise up against us and try to hurt our ministry. Even Christians have opposed us and hurled hurtful, untrue accusations at us.

---

[238] Psalm 62:6 KJV
[239] Luke 4:1-13
[240] Luke 4:14-30

You will get opposition and persecution also. Just like Elisha was blamed for the siege and the famine in Samaria,[241] you also may be blamed for things that aren't your fault. But, just as God protected Elisha from the murderous intent of the king, so also God will protect you.

Sometimes, the truth hurts.

As a blue-collar prophet, you have to tell the truth, and sometimes the truth is hard to hear. Sometimes, we have to confront things that aren't popular. In a couple of cases I've had to deal with adultery in the pastoral leadership of a church. Obviously, I'm not a popular guy afterward. It goes without saying, I don't get rebooked.

Sometimes people get angry. Sometimes they make threats. But, sometimes, they come around.

One time I prayed over a teenager who was dating the pastor's daughter. "You need to break up," I told him.

He was mad at me. But they broke up. (The pastor was happy.)

Even though he remained angry, his parents forced him to come to our meetings. Finally, months later, he stood up and gave this testimony.

"I used to hate Tom Stamman," he said. "But now I love him."

There will be people who literally hate you. Others will love you.

But, if people hate you, make sure they are hating you for the right reason. Some people are always

---

[241] 2 Kings 6:24-7:2

confronting, always exposing, always condemning, always telling people all their sins. If that's you, you don't have the gift of prophecy. You have the gift of criticism. As a rule, prophecies are for edification, exhortation and comfort. They are designed to bring healing, help and encouragement. Even Jesus, when He needed to correct the church, sandwiched his rebukes between words of encouragement.[242]

People sometimes reject prophetic words.

When I was praying over one lady, I said, "I see the word 'backsliding.' Have you ever backslid?"

She not only denied backsliding, but she got angry. She spoke with the pastor, and the pastor came to me. "You saw this lady backsliding," he said, "but she's just a brand new Christian. How does that relate?"

To be honest, I didn't know. One of the hardest things in the prophetic is to know what tense a word is in. Is it past, present or future? It can be very difficult to figure that out. Many times I don't know. This was one of those times.

Later the pastor came to me and said, "She did end up backsliding, so I guess the word was true."

The point is this: Sometimes people will reject, they will deny, they will question the words God gives you, but you must hold on to God, and trust the gift He has given you.

I was praying over a woman in Minnesota. God gave me five words for her. Each time I told her the word and asked her if the word made sense to her, she answered,

---

[242] See Revelation 2 & 3

"no." Finally, God said, *No matter what you say, she will say, "no."*

And, sure enough, she made it clear to me that the only reason she was there was to get me to pray for her mother's healing. She didn't want a word for herself.

Some people despise the prophetic.[243] Others are skeptical. You give them a word, and they say, "Of course you can figure that out."

I said to one man, "I see tires; I see motorcycle tires."

He said, "Well, of course, look at me!"

I said, "You may know that you have a motorcycle, but how would I know that?"

Some will complain that your words are too general. It is exciting when you get specific words for people -- occupation, name, prayer requests, whatever. But general words don't have less validity than specific words. Sometimes it isn't the *uniqueness* of the word, but the *timing* of the word that gives impact. For example, I might see the word "marriage problems." Every married couple has had challenges. So the word could apply to almost any married person. But, the power of this word might come from the current circumstances. For example, the wife might be planning to file for divorce the next day. This sort of thing has happened many times in our ministry. The word becomes a "stop sign" or a wake up call that can bring a radical change in direction.

Some people will test you. You may give them a word, and they will say, "You tell me what it means." You might have a word that's right on, but they want you to tell

---

[243]   1 Thessalonians 5:20

them what it means. God may give you the interpretation, and He may not. Don't be bothered by that.

God usually shows only a partial picture of what is going to happen. The scriptures are full of examples of people who received prophetic words that seem to be incomplete. For example, Moses was told that Pharaoh was going to resist letting the people of Israel go free, and God would bring signs and wonders to persuade Pharaoh to free them.[244] But God didn't share that it would take ten plagues and the splitting of the Red Sea before they would be totally free.[245] The people knew about the promised land, but God didn't reveal the dry times and the wandering in the wilderness for forty years. (Rumor has it, even back then, men wouldn't ask for directions.)

We live in a culture that can create challenges for the prophetic. Sometimes prophecies are delayed or do not come to pass.[246] This is a problem for people with a Western mindset. We like things to be cut and dried, exact and specific. We want answers now. Meditating and digging into God has been replaced by self-help, easy answer books. But Jesus spoke in parables, so people would have to seek Him, and draw near to Him before they could understand. Christ desires an intimate relationship with His bride. Sometimes, in order to establish a hunger for fellowship, He will share things that will cause us to seek Him more and more. We could learn much from Mary, the mother of Jesus, who received words about her Son that didn't make much sense at first, but she pondered

---

[244] Exodus 3:19-20
[245] Exodus 5-15
[246] For example, some prophecies are conditional. If conditions change, the outcome changes. See chapter 4.

these things in her heart.[247] She didn't dismiss these words. Instead, she waited on God to see what would happen.

In addition to these cultural challenges, some people can have powerful inner motivations for denying or rejecting the words God gives through you. One time I saw the word "adultery" over someone I prayed for. When I shared it, he denied it. A month later, he came back to me and said, "You know that word you had about a sexual sin? Well, it was true, but I was too embarrassed to admit it to anybody."

Embarrassment puts up walls. Lack of self-esteem can do the same thing. You may give an encouraging word, a leadership word, a word of victory and redemption. And the person you are praying for won't receive it. I prayed for a Native American. I told her, "I see you as a leader. I see great potential." But she wouldn't even pick up her chin. She was so beaten down by culture, and by her family that she could not believe the word. She denied it, because she could not bring herself to believe that God might do something special in her life.

The Bible says that our hearts are *deceitfully* wicked.[248] Some people are so accustomed to lying, that they lie to themselves and they believe the lie. Many times I've prayed over young people, and I've said something like, "I see a messy room."

The response, "Oh, no. It's not messy."

Meanwhile, the mother was saying, "What do you mean? You haven't cleaned it in years!"

---

[247]   Luke 2:19

[248]   Jeremiah 17:9

Some people will reject your words. Some will deny them. That may mean that you've made a mistake. Blue-collar prophets sometimes do make mistakes. But -- here's the key -- time will tell. Someday it will be clear whether you've made a mistake or the person is rejecting a word from God.

Watch out for the martyr complex.

Some prophets wear a chip on their shoulder, because people have rejected their words or their ministry. This results in a martyrdom complex or (as some call it) an "Elijah complex." Elijah fought against 850 devil worshippers and then ran from one woman.[249] Convinced he was the only person alive who was truly serving God,[250] he was so discouraged that he wanted to die.[251] The Lord spoke back and said, "I have 7,000 people who will not bow to Baal, quit feeling sorry for yourself. I have job for you to do."[252] Just because someone rejects you or your ministry does not give you the right to walk around with your tail between your legs. Keep your eyes on the Lord.

Let me share this with you: The church is not out to get you. Most believers are loving and kind and truly want to hear from God, so prophesy boldly.

My prophetic ministry was almost derailed before it got started.

One night, two years before I began my prophetic

---

[249] 1 Kings 18-19
[250] 1 Kings 19:10
[251] 1 Kings 19:4
[252] 1 Kings 19:15-18 paraphrased

ministry, I prayed for a couple of dozen people and shared with them what I sensed God was saying. I was excited about the results. A week later the pastor informed me that three of the words didn't make sense. Now I should have rejoiced about the twenty that did make sense, but instead I concentrated on my mistakes. I felt rejected and I said to myself I will never prophesy again. Thank God, even though I gave up, He didn't. In the summer of 1996, God showed up and the spirit of prophecy came over me and it hasn't left me since, praise God! But I had to learn to overcome rejection and feelings of failure when I made mistakes.

Be prepared to make mistakes and know that people are going to reject your words. Otherwise, you will walk with a wounded spirit that, unbeknownst to you, draws criticism and pain.

Get back in the saddle!

One of the most important things you can do when you have been hurt is to get back in the game and face the enemy. When I was in 3rd grade, I played Little League baseball. One evening I was facing a 7th grader pitcher. This guy was four years older than me and seemed as tall as Goliath. I was scared to death of him, and I was praying for a walk. The guy reared back and whipped the ball as hard as he could. The ball slammed into my arm, and I cringed in pain. In fact, I cried as I went to first base. The next day, my dad decided to give me some batting practice. He knew that I needed to get some practice, lest fear overtake me. So he gave me a bat and we went out in the yard. Now, if you think that 7th grader was tall, he was nothing compared to my dad. When my dad lobbed the ball toward me, I backed up like someone was trying to shoot me full of lead.

But my dad threw another pitch, and another, until my confidence came back and my fear left.

In the same way, your heavenly Father understands the pain of being rejected. When he sees people hurt you, he will give you more opportunities to minister. But He won't give you more than you can handle. We need to pick up our prophetic anointing "bat" and swing when the opportunities come our way.

Reverse the curse!

We've had psychics, Satanists, and New Age people come to our meetings to try to disrupt what the Spirit is doing. I've had people cuss and swear at me right in the service.

How do you respond when people do this? Jesus said, "Love your enemies and pray for those who persecute you."[253] Apart from any other guidance from the Lord, that is the place to start. Sometimes, however, the Lord wants us to reverse the curse. Consider Elisha's experience, soon after Elijah was taken into heaven:

> *23 From there Elisha went up to Bethel. As he was walking along the road, some youths came out of the town and jeered at him. "Go on up, you baldhead!" they said. "Go on up, you baldhead!" 24 He turned around, looked at them and called down a curse on them in the name of the Lord . Then two bears came out of the woods and mauled forty-two of the youths. 25 And he*

---

[253] Matthew 6:44

went on to Mount Carmel and from there returned to Samaria.[254]

Several things are important to understand about this incident. First, these were not little boys, but a gang of grown men, ages 18-25+. Second, this wasn't a joke. This was a deliberate attempt to intimidate and mock the Lord's prophet. They were testing God. This was spiritual rebellion and anarchy. God says, "Do not touch my anointed ones; do my prophets no harm."[255] The Lord takes this warning very seriously.

Third, these young men were cursing the Lord's prophet, and Elisha reversed the curse. A curse gives people a taste of hell just as a blessing gives people a taste of heaven. These youths met a bear on earth so they wouldn't have to meet an angry God in heaven.

In the New Testament, Paul, "filled with the Holy Spirit," looked at Elymas, the sorcerer, and said, "Now the hand of the Lord is against you. You are going to be blind, and for a time, you will be unable to see the light of the sun."[256] Elymas was trying to turn someone from the faith. But the Lord, through Paul, reversed the curse.

Likewise, there will be people who rise up and curse you. But God will give you insight into their designs[257] and the authority to reverse the curse.

Elijah ran from Jezebel partly because she cursed him by her gods.[258] Many people don't believe in curses.

---

[254] 2 Kings 2:23-25
[255] Psalm 105:15
[256] Acts:13:6-12
[257] See e.g., 2 Corinthians 2:11
[258] 1 Kings 19:2

But Balaam believed in curses, and God believed also, because He turned Balaam's curse into a blessing.[259]

My mom is a powerful prayer warrior. There was a bar in our home state that had a notorious reputation. Every Friday and Saturday night it was packed. Brawls, fights and all kinds of terrible things were happening there. She got sick of it. So she cursed it in the name of the Lord. It burned down that same night.

Can you imagine disobeying a mom like that?

By the way, the Lord may give blue-collar prophets a word of judgment for someone. I prayed for a guy with an addiction. I saw blood and violence. But he blew it off. I said, "If you don't change, you're going to go to jail." But he wouldn't take me seriously. Two years later, one of his friends was in a car, the car started on fire, and the friend was killed. The guy I prayed for was charged with murder. The word he didn't want to heed came true.

A glimpse into the spirit world shows us why we have mercy on our enemies.

Only rarely do we get a clear view into the spirit world to see what is going on all around us. One of the most interesting episodes of this type occurred when Elisha prayed that the eyes of his servant might be opened to see what God was doing when Elisha was surrounded by enemies. Here's the story from 2 Kings 6:

> *8 Now the king of Aram was at war with Israel. After conferring with his*

---

[259] Deuteronomy 23:4-5

officers, he said, "I will set up my camp in such and such a place."

9 The man of God sent word to the king of Israel: "Beware of passing that place, because the Arameans are going down there."

10 So the king of Israel checked on the place indicated by the man of God. Time and again Elisha warned the king, so that he was on his guard in such places.

11 This enraged the king of Aram. He summoned his officers and demanded of them, "Will you not tell me which of us is on the side of the king of Israel?"

12 "None of us, my lord the king," said one of his officers, "but Elisha, the prophet who is in Israel, tells the king of Israel the very words you speak in your bedroom."

13 "Go, find out where he is," the king ordered, "so I can send men and capture him." The report came back: "He is in Dothan."

14 Then he sent horses and chariots and a strong force there. They went by night and surrounded the city.

15 When the servant of the man of God got up and went out early the next morning, an army with horses and chariots had surrounded the city. "Oh, my lord, what shall we do?" the servant asked.

16 "Don't be afraid," the prophet answered. "Those who are with us are more than those who are with them."

17 And Elisha prayed, "O Lord , open his eyes so he may see." Then the Lord opened the servant's eyes, and he looked and saw the hills full of horses and chariots of fire all around Elisha.

18 As the enemy came down toward him, Elisha prayed to the Lord , "Strike these people with blindness." So he struck them with blindness, as Elisha had asked.

19 Elisha told them, "This is not the road and this is not the city. Follow me, and I will lead you to the man you are looking for."

And he led them to Samaria.

20 After they entered the city, Elisha said, "Lord , open the eyes of these men so they can see." Then the Lord opened their eyes and they looked, and there they were, inside Samaria.

21 When the king of Israel saw them, he asked Elisha, "Shall I kill them, my father? Shall I kill them?"

22 "Do not kill them," he answered. "Would you kill men you have captured with your own sword or bow? Set food and water before them so that they may eat and drink and then go back to their master." 23 So he prepared a great feast for them, and after they had finished eating and drinking, he sent them away, and they returned to their master. So the bands from Aram stopped raiding Israel's territory.

Just as God showed Elisha what the enemy was up to, God will show you what people are trying to do. He will show the plan of the enemy. For example, I prayed over a girl in Iowa, and I said, "The devil's plan for you is to get pregnant before you get married. So break up with this guy." She didn't listen. She got pregnant. Other times I've prayed over pastors, and said, "People are going to rise up against you. Stand strong, and the Lord will be on your side." And sure enough, it happened. People rose up against the man of God. He stood his ground because of that prophetic word, and God turned it around for good.

God may give you a view into the spirit world so you too can see that "those who are with us are more than those who are with them." When we begin to understand this, it becomes much easier to show love and help our human enemy and send him on his way. God is our shield and our protector, and will help us overcome our real enemy, the devil. Remember that "our struggle is not against flesh and blood, but against . . . the spiritual forces of evil . . ."[260]

Moving in the prophetic may stir up Satanic opposition and persecution. That is true. But, if persecution takes place, the prophetic gift can be wonderfully used by God to bring glory to God's name.

God uses the prophetic to strengthen and encourage His children in times of persecution

One Sunday morning a few years ago, a violent

---

[260] Ephesians 6:12

mob, shouting and screaming, gathered around a Christian ministry in India.

The director of the ministry went out and tried to calm the crowd. "Why are you here?" he said. "We Christians stand for peace. We mean you no harm."

The crowd, armed with sticks and knives, refused to listen to the director. Instead, they grabbed him and began beating him with sticks.

Watching all of this was the director's little girl, a child of almost two, barely able to speak. She was so young that she never put more than a word or two together. When she saw her daddy being beaten, she knew something was wrong and so she began walking toward her father.

One of the Christian women saw the child. Instantly, she realized that the child's life was in terrible danger. The mob, intoxicated with violence, would kill this little girl without a second thought. So the woman ran and swooped up the child. Immediately the crowd turned on her. They chased her to the women's building, but she made it inside with the child and bolted the door behind her.

The women inside the building were beside themselves with fear. They locked the windows as the crowd outside became more and more frenzied in their attempts to break in or burn the building down. But, in the midst of their screams, they heard a voice speaking to them.

It was the little child.

"Why are you afraid?" she asked.

Somehow the child's sudden gift of speech caught the frightened women off guard and silenced them. Then the little one spoke again.

"Don't you know that you are the apple of My eye?"

God spoke through a little child. And, for these

terrified women, screams gave way to songs of worship as the presence and peace of God entered that building.

Though the mob repeatedly doused the house with kerosene and tried to set it ablaze, they were not successful, and they finally gave up in frustration.[261]

God will give wisdom to know how to deal with persecutors.

I knew a man who had to deal with a bully at work. Every time he went to work, this guy would pick on him. So he prayed about it, and God showed him what to say. The next day, he went to work, and the guy picked on him again. So he said, "P rayed last night, and God wants to know why you don't talk to Him any more."

The bully replied, "Because you talk to Him so much, He doesn't have time to listen to me." And he walked away.

Later that day, the bully came back and said, "How did you know I used to talk to God." And he never bothered him again.

After the break up of the Soviet Union, a team of young people from Russia made an evangelism trip into the former Soviet Republic of Kazakhstan. While witnessing on the streets of the main city in Kazakhstan, they were arrested by the police. At the police station, they were interrogated and beaten. Most of them were women. They were treated with obscenity and violation of one kind or another. They were put in jail. At night they were brought

---

[261] From an account given by Indian Missionary Sam Dharam to an audience at Lake City Church, Madison, Wisconsin on 10/17/1999.

back out to be subjected to the same kind of treatment, night after night for several days.

Behind this persecution was the police chief, a great big burly guy. He said, "I hate Christians. I don't believe there is a God. I don't want anybody talking about God on the streets of our city. And I hate Russians, because Russians were our oppressors during the days of the Soviet Union." He was a Kazak, and he saw an opportunity to express his ethnic hatred against these Russian kids.

Finally, he dragged the team leader, a 23-year-old Russian woman, into his office. He threw her down into a chair and said, "Today, you die. Your parents will never know what happened to you. We're good at making people disappear, just like your people did to us. I have people out there loading their guns right now. You are going to die, and we are going to dispose of your body. You'll never see your parents again."

But this 23-year old woman had been unaffected during all the days of this abuse. When she heard she was going to die, she looked at this big police chief, and she said, "Do you know what your problem is? When you were six years old, this happened to you. And when you were twelve, this happened. And when you were fifteen, you went through this." She started reading this guy's mail and telling him what his life had been like, in vivid detail.

He said, "Who told you that stuff? How did you know these things about me?"

She said, "God told me, because there not only is a God, but He loves you."

This man started to weep like a baby, and wept so hard that he started shaking and fell out of his chair onto the floor, on his knees and repented. He asked God to come into his life and have mercy on him. Now he's a pastor overseeing five churches.[262]

---

[262] From an account presented to an audience at Lake City Church, Madison, Wisconsin on 6/9/2001.

CHAPTER 8:

Practical wisdom for the blue-collar prophet

What went wrong?

The doctor shook his head. "No," he said, "I'm sorry, but your daughter *needs* surgery."

The baby girl's father rocked his daughter gently in his arms. "I don't expect you to believe me," he said to the doctor. "You can schedule surgery. But I believe you are going to tell me that she doesn't need it."

"Look," replied the doctor, "I have seen genuine miracles in other countries around the world. But they usually don't happen here. Your daughter needs surgery."

The dad just smiled. *I know something you don't,* he thought to himself. *I have a personal prophecy, in writing, assuring me that the Lord will heal my daughter. This prophecy assures me that the doctor will agree with me that she doesn't need surgery.*

This father walked out of the doctor's office with a smile on his face. He went out and enlisted many people to pray for his daughters healing -- not because he doubted the word, but because he wanted as many people as possible to share in the joy of answered prayer.

The day of surgery came. *No problem,* he thought. *God often waits to the last moment.*

The nurses wheeled her away to the surgical suite.

This is cutting it close, he thought, but he sat down with confidence in the surgical waiting room.

Any moment now. "*We can't figure it out,*" *they will say.* "*When we took your daughter in, she had a club foot. When we went to operate, her foot was perfectly normal.*"

Any moment now.

Five hours passed. When the surgeon came in, he looked tired but satisfied. "She came through the surgery fine," he said. "You'll be able to see her in about an hour."

In the place of a perfect foot was a blood-soaked cast. In the place of big, bright baby eyes, were frightened eyes, dull with pain. There was a healing, but it was a clumsy human healing, far removed from the Divine miracle that had been predicted.[263]

What went wrong?

Bill Hamon, who has written a number of books on prophecy and has one of the top prophetic ministries in America, advises prophets to avoid prophesying about certain things. Healing is one of those things.

Here's the reason: When we let our doctrine dictate our prophetic words, we open ourselves up to mistakes in the prophetic. We know according to God's Word, that God wants to heal people. However, for some reason -- and there are reasons -- some people don't get healed. Elisha was sick -- he didn't get healed. If you mix your theology in with your prophecy, you make mistakes.

I pray for healing. I believe God for healing. But I

---

[263] This incident happened to co-author Dwight Clough and his daughter Liza in 1991.

don't prophesy healings, because if they don't happen, I lose credibility, the prophetic loses credibility, and God's name can be damaged.

In Greek, there are two words for "word," - *logos* and *rhema*. While the *logos* has to do with the written word, *rhema* has a different meaning. It involves a divinely inspired impression in your soul, a flash of thought or a creative idea from God, deeper assurance and a witness of the Spirit.

Bill Hamon points out: "The main cause of this problem is that the person often prophesies from the *logos* and not from a *rhema*... We can preach, confess, quote and stand on the *logos*, but we cannot make it into a personal prophecy to an individual unless the Holy Spirit has quickened it into a *rhema*."[264] For example, we can preach that according to God's Word "by His stripes we are healed,"[265] in the same way we are saved by faith, but we must not confuse this with a *rhema* word. I have found, however, that, if God reveals a sickness supernaturally, I can almost assure the person that God is going to heal them.

Be careful when you minister prophetically to not let your opinions become God's will for others.   For example, I have strong opinions about sending my children to Christian school as opposed to sending them to public school.   If you have strong opinions about something, label them as opinions, not as prophecies.   Let people know that you are giving them a word from your heart, not a word

---

[264]   Bill Hamon, *Prophets and Personal Prophecy*, pp. 39-40
[265]   Isaiah 53:5, 1 Peter 2:24

from the Lord.[266]

If you have a strong emotional attachment to something, then be careful about sharing a word. For example, if I see a child being molested, my emotions tell me to throw the molester in jail and throw away the key. I'm probably not the best one to prophesy over that child molester.

Take care that you are not pressured by others to manufacture a prophetic word to their liking. Even if what they want you to say is right on. For example, I'm dealing with a situation where a son is in rebellion against his dad. Of course, I volunteered to pray and prophesy over the son. But I must be careful to prophesy *only* what the Lord tells me, *not* what his dad wants me to tell him.[267]

Sometimes, if I know too much about a situation, I won't even touch that area, because I know too much. I'll just say, "You know what - I know too much - it's probably best if you don't ask me to prophesy about that circumstance."

Don't prophesy whom to marry. Don't say, "Here, marry this person." Don't predict that a backslider will come back to God or a divorced person will come back to a marriage. You can't guarantee these things, because people have a free choice.

Remember, Prophecy has the power to give life or death depending on how you use it. So walk in caution, but not in fear.

---

[266] 1 Corinthians 7:10, 12
[267] See e.g., 1 Kings 22:6-28

Submit to the Word of God.

To be a prophet of the Lord, you must recognize that the Word of God is true and follow the principles of prophesying according to the Word of God.[268] If you submit to God's Word, God will shield you from deception.[269] One of the most important safeguards to prevent a child of God from becoming a diviner or fortune teller is to believe and practice the written Word of God. All, and, I repeat, all prophecies *must* line up with God's Word or you are a false prophet. Our ultimate prophetic handbook is God's Word. Under no circumstances can we allow ourselves to be tempted to sever our ties from God's Holy Word. If you have serious doubts of the authenticity of the Word of God, then I advise you to read Christian apologetic books that defend the integrity and the full inspiration of God's Scriptures, and I heartily encourage you to avoid the prophetic lest you fall into the trap of the enemy.

Don't be afraid to start small

Don't be afraid to start small. The Bible says not to despise small beginnings.[270] General words may appear on the surface as insignificant, because they apply to anyone. However, God can use them to prick the heart. God can use them to change a life. This will ultimately result in praise and glory to God. Furthermore, if I am faithful in sharing simple or general words, I have found that God may

---

[268] "If anyone thinks himself to be a prophet or spiritually gifted, let him acknowledge that what I am writing to you is the Lord's command." -- 1 Corinthians 14:37
[269] See, e.g., Proverbs 30:5-6
[270] Zechariah 4:10

then give more specific and detailed words.

One way to start in blue-collar prophecy is to prophesy over your children or your spouse. They won't think you're a fruitcake. Because you know them, you can be confident. You'll probably also get the interpretation right because you know your family.

Jacob prophesied over his sons.[271] He knew his sons, but that didn't stop him from prophesying. Some of the best words I've ever had are for people I know really well. I was talking to my wife once over the phone. I said, "Honey, I see all these balloons." And here she was doodling on a telephone book, drawing balloons.

One time I was talking to my wife and I saw the name of a city I had preached at in Illinois, the name "Pekin." God revealed to her what that meant. When one of the children was little, she used to look at him when he was in the crib and she would say, "I'm peekin' at you." God showed her He was doing the same thing with her, He was "peekin'" at her. He was keeping His eye on her, just as she was keeping an eye on that little boy in that crib.

The Lord gives me words for my children also. One of my daughters is always asking for words from God. And many of them have come to pass. One time she didn't have any friends. I prayed and said, "God is going to give you friends." That year, she got a friend. And now, she has friends all over the country. She's president of her class. She's on the basketball team and the volleyball team. She's becoming a leader, and she has great friends. But, at the time I originally prophesied, she didn't have a single friend.

---

[271] Genesis 49:1-28

Get a mentor and stay accountable.

You need a mentor, someone to watch over you, to protect you, to pray over you. Sometimes you need to run prophecies by someone before you share them. Elisha had Elijah as a mentor. The company of the prophets apparently provided some type of training or mentoring.[272]

Beware of the lone ranger mentality. You may envision yourself as an Elijah, walking alone with God and being used mightily of God. But even Elijah had his struggles, and you will too. When you are alone it is far too easy to fall into discouragement, depression and possibly deception. We need each other. Jesus knew that, and that's why He sent people out two by two.

Every prophet needs a pastor and every pastor needs a prophet. Not only that but every prophet needs other prophets to keep them in line. David was a prophet.[273] He spoke many Messianic prophecies.[274]

Yet David surrounded himself with prophets like Nathan and Gad.[275] Paul states, "Two or three prophets should speak, and the others should weigh carefully what is said."[276] In the early church, each local church had more than one prophet. The Bible says that matters are established by the testimony of two or three witnesses.[277]

---

[272] See, e.g., 2 Kings 2:3, 9:1
[273] Acts 2:29-30
[274] E.g., Psalm 22
[275] 2 Samuel 7:4, 24:11; 1 Chronicles 21:9, 29:9 etc.
[276] 1 Corinthians 14:29
[277] Deuteronomy 19:15, Matthew 18:16, 2 Corinthians 13:1 etc.

By surrounding yourself with other prophetic men and women of God, you will build in safeguards to protect yourself. I have also found that it is easier to hear God for others than to hear God for yourself. Therefore, I look forward to prophetic words for myself from other prophetic people to verify my thoughts, dreams and intentions.

The company of the prophets had Elisha as a covering.[278] He served as a protection for them. You need a covering. You need to run your plans and prophecies by your pastor. If you attend a church that doesn't believe in the prophetic, go find a church that does, or keep attending the church you are at, but get under a seasoned prophetic ministry.

It is very dangerous to try to prophesy and move in the gifts of the Spirit without a covering. Harold Eatmon, a brother who has moved in the prophetic for 20+ years, said to me, "The prophetic and psychic are very similar, and there's a gray area that you can cross over into the psychic. That's why you need a covering." You need a pastor; you need a shepherd. Prophets and kings always worked together in the Old Testament. Nathan was a prophet, but he bowed before King David.[279] Even though he confronted David after the sin with Bathsheba,[280] he still had honor and respect for the king. Prophets need to be under authority.

The Bible says, first there's apostles, then there's prophets.[281] It doesn't say first prophets, then apostles. There's somebody above a prophet. You need somebody

---

[278] 2 Kings 9:1
[279] 1 Kings 1:23
[280] 2 Samuel 12:7
[281] 1 Corinthians 12:28

above you. There are some people who walk into a church and say, "Thus saith the Lord, 'There's Ichabod all over the church. You're all backslidden and all messed up.'" But these prophets are not under authority. I would not receive a prophecy from someone who is not under authority.

Everyone needs to be under authority. I'm under authority. I have a board. I have a pastor who watches over me. Prays over me. Keeps me in line. I'm part of a denomination. If I start getting weird, they'll give me the left foot of fellowship. Everybody needs a covering. Otherwise, you're going to be like a bowl of granola -- fruity, flaky and nutty. Speaking of cereal, last week Snap, Crackle and Pop were killed -- by a cereal killer.

Avoid misunderstandings.

Sooner or later, people will misinterpret your prophetic words. Count on it.

I was in a church in Minnesota. I had the pastor next to me for accountability, and for protection. I saw this person having a will. I said, "When's the last time you made out a will?"

She answered, "1965."

I said, "I think you're due for one. Get a will. I'm not saying that anyone is going to die right away. So don't think you're going to die. Don't go home and panic. But do get a will. It's just a wise thing to do. All right? But again, don't worry about anybody dying."

What did she do? She went home to her husband and said, "The prophet says you are going to die, so we need to get a will."

Of course, he got upset. Because he was upset, he called his pastor. His pastor called the pastor of the church where I was at. "What is this?!" he wanted to know, and he explained what his congregant had told him.

Thank God the pastor was there, overheard the prophecy and was able to clear the whole thing up. But, as an additional safeguard, I got it on tape.

We try to tape the prophecies or have people write them down. That way you can prove what you said. You can tape record the prophetic words on a master tape and then separate them, or tape each individual word and hand it to the person that received the prayer. Or you can have someone write it down, or write it down yourself immediately after the word. That way the person will remember what you told them. You can verify its accuracy. And, if needed, you can run the prophecy by someone else first before you give it.

Working with pastors

Since 1986, I've preached over 3,500 times at churches across North America. I have also served as a youth pastor, and worked on staff with various pastors. I know what most experienced Christian workers know: It is relatively easy for Satan to cause problems between sincere believers.

It comes as no surprise that one of the most common problems in the prophetic is working with pastors.

God wants His leaders to get along. He has given us Biblical principles and wisdom from the Spirit to accomplish this. Take heed to these insights.

#1. Your pastor is not your enemy. He is designed by God to give guidance, protection and love to the sheep. Assuming he is a believer in the Scriptures, then your pastor knows the numerous warnings that Jesus and Paul gave about wolves in sheep's clothing. Time and time again the authors of Scripture from Moses to John warn covenant believers that there are false prophets; therefore any shepherd worth his weight will be on the lookout for people who may fit the profile of a false prophet. If the shepherd does not guard the flock of God, then he will have to answer to God on the day of judgment. If you understand the weight of responsibility the shepherd has before God, then you will not get offended if the pastor has some guidelines before you share with someone privately, or if you share openly in the church. That leads us to ...

#2. Get permission first. Remember you are a mailman, if the postmaster tells the mailman to change his route, then he should obey him. If a pastor tells you it is the wrong time, or not to share, then release it to God. As a mailman you did your duty, now the pastor will have to answer to his supervisor, i.e. God. It is highly unethical to try to minister to people in a prophetic voice inside the church walls, or parking lot without the pastor's permission. When I attended a revival in Missouri, no one was allowed to prophesy, so even though we have an established ministry, I obeyed their rules. Later, when we went out to eat, I got a chance to minister to a number of people.

#3. Don't be a bash-and-dash prophet. Some self-proclaimed prophets walk into a service and bash the body and then dart out. Others will write unsigned notes and put it in a pastor's brief case or mail him an unsigned letter. If you don't have enough confidence and boldness to sign your name, then keep your mouth shut.

#4. You can develop trust by serving and hanging around other anointed people. Just as you can be guilty by association, you can get people to trust you, if you are being mentored or trained by a person who has a proven track record. Be like Elisha and become a servant at your own expense and watch God begin to give you favor. If pastors see you helping and serving a proven minister it will help them trust you.

#5. Pray for your pastor, and the other pastors you work with.

#6. A spoon full of sugar goes further than a gallon of vinegar.

#7. Stay humble. Remember, you could be wrong. Prophets do make mistakes.

#8. Take the time to earn their trust.

#9. Sometimes, a prophet is not welcome in his own hometown.[282] You may have to prophesy elsewhere.

#10. Get letters of recommendation from other pastors. They can open doors like no one else.

#11. Before I share a word with the church I generally run it by the pastor.

#12. Don't be eager to rebuke an elder.[283] If you must do so, do it privately.

#13. Just because someone is a pastor, doesn't mean he is immune from insecurity, competition or jealousy.[284]

#14. Remember, we need to submit one to another.[285]

Timing, a key to the prophetic

One of the keys to the prophetic is waiting for the right time. When Elijah fled from Jezebel and met the Lord

---

[282] Luke 4:24

[283] 1 Timothy 5:1

[284] See 1 Kings 13 for an account of how jealousy-inspired lying destroyed a prophetic ministry.

[285] Ephesians 5:21

in the wilderness, the Lord told Elijah to anoint three leaders[286]:

1. Elisha to succeed Elijah as prophet.
2. Hazael to be king of Aram.
3. Jehu to be king of Israel.

But, if you continue reading, you'll discover that Elijah only anointed one of those people, i.e., Elisha[287]. Hazael was anointed much later by Elisha[288]. Jehu was anointed by an unnamed prophet designated by Elisha[289].

All of these anointings were an outgrowth of Elijah's ministry. Yet God enabled him to discern the timing. And when the right time came, it was Elijah's successors that did the anointing.

One of the keys of moving in the prophetic is to ask God, "Am I supposed to share this prophetic word, or am I just supposed to pray quietly for these people?"

There is a time for everything.[290] There are times to prophesy and times to refrain. Prophecy, for example, should not interrupt the flow of the service.[291] Some people want to prophesy over a waitress when she has 80 tables to wait on. That's not right.

Find a convenient way to prophesy. For example, don't try to prophesy over someone in the middle of a service. I've had people do that to me. "I have a word for you, Tom." They want to give me a word, and I'm trying to worship God, or I'm preparing my sermon, or it's twelve

---

[286] 1 Kings 19:15-17
[287] 1 Kings 19:19-21
[288] 2 Kings 8:7-15
[289] 2 Kings 9:1-13
[290] Ecclesiastes 3:1
[291] 1 Corinthians 14:31-33

o'clock at night -- I still have a four hour drive ahead of me to get home.

Mail it to me!

Take turns. God desires that all of his believers prophesy. Sadly, some believers hog the show and they do all of the prophesying. There have been numerous instances in which I have prayed for someone and the words that I am sharing do not seem to hit home. Then the pastor or the prayer warrior next to me will get a word or an interpretation and the recipient will brighten up and begin to praise God because of the encouraging word and prophecy from someone other than myself. It is an awesome and exhilarating experience to be used of God, so grant others the opportunity to use their gifts.

People often ask, "Does it always flow?" People will say, I want to go out to eat with Tom because he might get a word for me or something like that. No, it does not always flow. You can turn it on, and you can turn it off. Otherwise, you'd never be able to sleep at night if it ran 24 hours a day.

Pray first.

Nathan was a great prophet of the Lord. But even he made a mistake when he neglected to pray first.[292] Before Daniel shared a word, he took time to pray.[293] John rested on Jesus' chest. He was known as the beloved disciple. No wonder God used him to write over twenty

---

[292] 2 Samuel 7:1-16
[293] Daniel 2:16-19

chapters of prophecy in the Bible. If we rest on Jesus, we will feel His pulse, hear His heart, and be able to speak His mind.

Watch their eyes.

The lamp of the body is the eye. If therefore your eye is good, your whole body will be full of light. But if your eye is bad, your whole body will be full of darkness. If therefore the light that is in you is darkness, how great is that darkness![294]

Another key in the prophetic is watching people's eyes. The eyes are the windows to the soul. I was praying over a man, and I saw addictions. I looked into his eyes, and I knew it was lust. I brought him off to the side[295] and I said, "I see lust." He admitted that he was into pornography and had been for a long time. But he repented, and I gave him a word of wisdom on what to do to overcome it. Then he asked me, "How could you tell?"

I said, "I could see it in your eyes."

He said, "Can other people see it in my eyes?"

I said, "I don't know if other people can, but I can."

You can see a lot in other people's eyes. You can see joy. You can see depression . Sometimes someone is smiling on the outside, but their eyes are sad. Ask God to give you eyes to see what can't be seen. I can see demons

---

[294] Matthew 6: 22 -23

[295] Remember, if you have words that are embarrassing to people, don't preach over a microphone. You can screw up somebody's life. If the issue has to do with marriage, divorce, sex or other personal, sensitive matters, always take the person off to the side.

in people's eyes. It's really strange. But I've seen schizophrenia in some people by watching their eyes; as I speak to them their eyes dart to the right and to the left. I can tell when people are lying, because I ask them a question and then they look up or look sideways to decide how to answer. Then I know they are ducking the question.

Outward appearance

Hannah was being tormented by her husband's other wife, because she could not have children. When Eli, the priest, saw Hannah sobbing in the temple, he assumed by outward appearances that she was drunk.[296] Thank the Lord, she wasn't easily offended by Eli's spiritual insensitivity. But how many times have we misjudged a person or denounced a person because of outward problems?

A number of years ago I went to a youth rally in southern Minnesota. I walked in and was amazed at how chaotic, and out of hand things were. Kids were talking and goofing around during the worship time. One young man was walking around talking to girls during the service. When he finished talking to one girl, he went to talk to another . I was agitated in my spirit, so I pulled him out of the service, and I saw the word "abandoned by his father." He was touched by that, and he had tears in his eyes. He went back, sat down, and behaved himself. Another young man was also disturbing the worship service by talking to girls and goofing around. I pulled him out, chatted with him, and I said, "I see a sexual battering ram" --not a very positive word. I saw a spirit of lust on him. "Calm

---

[296] 1 Samuel 1:9-17

yourself down and behave yourself," I said.

Later, when it was time for prayer, people lined up to get prayed for. Although there were four prayer lines, mine was by far the longest, even though I wasn't the one preaching. These two boys were recruiting people to come to me for prayer. They were telling all their friends to line up for prayer.

While the rest of the rally moved into a concert, I prayed for twenty to thirty of the most rebellious, bad-attitude kids. These two boys who had been collared, were the ones bringing them up to me for prayer. They brought all the tough, in-your-face kids, and God moved mightily in revival. We saw kids delivered from demons. I saw a spirit of suicide over one kid. When I told him, he admitted he was planning to kill himself that week. He got delivered. A few kids got saved. The power of God fell. Some of the religious people didn't like it, but God sure did.

One of the most difficult things to overcome in the prophetic is judging people by their age, looks, countenance, dress, where they are seated in the sanctuary, and so on. A man in his early thirties attended one of our meetings in Wisconsin. During the preaching time he looked extremely bored and acted very skeptical. His hair was messed up and he was wearing sweats. The word I received was "pastoring in the pasture." I had no idea what it meant. After I shared the word, I stood there dumbfounded. Praise God, the man spoke up and told me that he was a pastor of a church. I want to let you know that the man did not look or act like a pastor and it would have been tempting to go by an outward appearance, but the Lord knows the heart. We have to be careful not to write people off because of their age, occupation or looks. As Ray Boltz sang, "For when others see a shepherd boy, God may see a king."

Try, try again.

When the son born to the Shunammite woman died, Elisha was called upon to intervene.[297]   He instructed Gehazi to lay his staff on the boy to raise him from the dead, but that prophetic instruction didn't produce results.[298] Most people would have given up. Not Elisha. He got personally involved, prayed to the Lord, and the Lord honored his tenacity.[299] Elisha even admitted that the Lord had hidden from him the fact that the boy was dead. Even Old Testament prophets were limited. Nobody knows it all. Paul said, "We prophesy in part, and we know in part."[300]

On the bench for Jesus?

There are going to be times when you're not on center stage. There were forty-three years of silence in Elisha's life, where the Bible tells us nothing about what he was doing.[301] There were similar gaps in Biblical coverage in the lives of Daniel, Paul, Moses and even Jesus.

There are also going to be dry times. God may put you on the bench for a while. There are times when God will prune you. And work on your character. And so, during that time, don't think the Spirit has left you. God

---

[297]   2 Kings 4:18-37
[298]   2 Kings 4:29-31
[299]   2 Kings 4:32-35, see also 2 Kings 2:4-14
[300]   1 Corinthians 13:8
[301]   Study 2 Kings 13:14-20 in the context of the chronology of the kings of Israel and Judah

may be doing some character work. He may be emphasizing something different.

I prayed over a man in South Dakota who had just graduated from Bible school. I saw him and his family taking a vacation in the Black Hills. He is an extremely intense person. He said, "I want to know what ministry I'm called to."

But I said, "You don't need to know right now. Right now just have fun with your family."

"But I want to know." He almost had tears in his eyes because he thought God didn't want to call him, and he thought God didn't have a plan for him.

"God does have a plan for you," I told him. "You're so intense, you need to take a break and have fun."

"Well, I want to be in the ministry."

"I know you want to be in the ministry, but there are times when you just need to take a break. You need a Sabbatical."

How ministries grow

Remember the man who was given a mina.[302] He invested that mina and earned five more. What did he get as a reward? His reward was not minas, but cities.[303] He gave the coins to the Master and was given charge of five cities. He was faithful with little coins and was given cities. That's called exponential blessing and anointing. We're faithful with little things for a season. I've seen people serve and help and nothing's happening. You may buy this book, seek the prophetic anointing, and, at first

---

[302] I.e., about three month's wages
[303] Luke 19:18-19

nothing happens. But you keep on being faithful, and one day -- BOOM!! -- it happens!

When I was 17 years old I saw the prophetic in action and I wanted to be like that. But it didn't come right away. I was faithful in Bible School. I was faithful in serving God. I was faithful in teaching churches how to witness. Eighteen years later the anointing hit me. It was powerful, and it changed my whole ministry.

And remember that multiplication is our goal. God has called prophets, just like other leaders, to equip the saints to do the work of the ministry. One of your goals is to equip other blue-collar prophets. One prophet can only do so much. But a hundred prophets can do a hundred times more.

Chapter 9:

Biblical perspectives, definitions, questions and answers

Is it really for today?

Many sincere, wonderful, committed, on-fire Christians do not believe that God speaks through the prophetic today. They usually support this idea with this Scripture:

> *8Love never fails. But where there are prophecies, they will cease; where there are tongues, they will be stilled; where there is knowledge, it will pass away. 9For we know in part and we prophesy in part, 10but when perfection comes, the imperfect disappears. 11When I was a child, I talked like a child, I thought like a child, I reasoned like a child. When I became a man, I put childish ways behind me. 12Now we see but a poor reflection as in a mirror; then we shall see face to face. Now I know in part; then I shall know fully, even as I am*

fully known.[304]

The argument goes like this: According to this passage of Scripture, prophecies will cease. There is no need for prophecies because we have the written Bible. Prophets and prophecies ceased to exist when the Bible was canonized.[305] The Bible is perfect. Since perfection has come (i.e., Scripture has been canonized), there is no need for prophecy and it has ceased.

These are sincere objections, and they deserve honest consideration. Let me respond. Understand, first of all, I want to advance the cause of Christ by not arguing with my born-again brothers and sisters. I want to lovingly support other Christians who spread the gospel, even those who disagree with me.

With that in mind, let's take another look at this passage. Many scholars believe that the phrase "when perfection comes" refers to the return of Jesus Christ. That explanation makes much more sense to me. Even though the Bible is perfect, nothing else is perfect in this life. Only the Second Coming will bring true perfection.

"When perfection comes" three things must happen: (1) prophecies will cease, (2) tongues will be stilled, (3) knowledge will pass away. All three are to happen when perfection comes. Did knowledge cease?

If knowledge has ceased, how do you know?

You can't have two gifts pass away, but not knowledge. All three gifts -- prophecies, tongues, and

---

[304] 1 Corinthians 13:8-12

[305] Canonization was the process in which the church came into agreement which books were inspired and which ones weren't. This process took place in the fourth century AD.

knowledge -- will pass away. If one gift hasn't passed away, then neither have the other two gifts passed away.

When we have a passage of Scripture, like this one, where the meaning isn't crystal clear to everyone, we must interpret this passage in light of other Scriptures that are abundantly clear. Consider this passage:

> *In the last days, God says,*
> *I will pour out my Spirit on all people.*
> *Your sons and daughters will prophesy,*
> *your young men will see visions,*
> *your old men will dream dreams.*
> *Even on my servants, both men and women,*
> *I will pour out my Spirit in those days,*
> *and they will prophesy.*[306]

Are we living in the last days? Most Christians agree to that. In fact, the Bible proves that we are. Peter quoted this passage from Joel[307] to explain what was happening on the Day of Pentecost. If Peter was in the last days 2000 years ago, then we certainly must be in the last days today.

While the written word (*logos*) of God is complete, we still need to hear words (*rhema*) from God's voice, from time to time. Someone explained it to me like this: "As a minister I preach the *logos*, but as a prophet I prophesy the *rhema*.[308] . . . General biblical truth does not guarantee

---

[306] Acts 2:17-18
[307] Joel 2:28-29
[308] "Rhema denotes that which is spoken, what is uttered in speech and writing: in the singular, a word. The significance of rhema (as

171

specific application and appropriation of that truth. A preacher speaks the letter of the Word which applies to all men for all time, while the prophet speaks from the Spirit of the Word which is personalized to a particular person for a specific situation."[309]

Some claim that the following passage shows that prophets are no longer part of God's plan:

> *1In the past God spoke to our forefathers through the prophets at many times and in various ways, 2but in these last days he has spoken to us by his Son, whom he appointed heir of all things, and through whom he made the universe.*[310]

These people say that once Jesus Christ appeared on

---

distinct from logos) is exemplified in the injunction to take 'the sword of the Spirit, which is the word (rhema) of God' (Ephesians 6:17). Here the reference is not to the whole Bible as such, but to the individual scripture which the Spirit brings to our remembrance for use in time of need, a prerequisite being the regular storing of the mind with scripture." -- W.E. Vine, An Expository Dictionary of New Testament Words, Nashville, TN, Nelson, 193, p. 1242

[309] I copied this quote, but I'm unsure of the source. The source may be Bill Hamon, and I certainly do recommend his books.

[310] Hebrews 1:1-2

the scene, there no longer was a need for prophets.

Again, we must consider the context of all Scripture. If this argument were true, then why didn't the Bible end with the four Gospels? Jesus Himself answers that question:

> *12"I have much more to say to you, more than you can now bear. 13But when he, the Spirit of truth, comes, he will guide you into all truth. He will not speak on his own; he will speak only what he hears, and he will tell you what is yet to come.*[311]

That's why there were prophets in the early church[312] and there continue to be prophets in the church today. In fact, the church is built on the foundation of apostles and prophets,[313] not theologians and seminarians. Prophets have an important role in the church. One of the last verses in the Bible refers to prophets.[314] We acknowledge the role of pastors, teachers and evangelists. Why is it difficult to acknowledge the role of prophets?

Hundreds of times in the Bible, people asked prophets for advice, counsel and direction.[315] One of the biggest struggles for Christians is knowing the will of God. That is because we make thousands of decisions in our lives where the Bible does not give specific guidance. Does that mean God is uninterested in what decision we

---

[311]   John 16:12-13
[312]   Acts 11:27, 13:1, 15:32, 21:10; 1 Corinthians 14:29, etc.
[313]   Ephesians 2:20
[314]   Revelation 22:9
[315]   1 Samuel 9:9 etc.

make?

The Bible gives us direction on many topics from marriage to ministry, but there are some areas where God's will is not clearly defined. For example, which Christian should you marry?[316] Where should you work? Should you move? Which college should you attend? Which born-again church should you go to? What type of ministry should you be involved in? The Spirit of God wants to speak into our lives on these issues.

But even if there were no "practical" reason for God to give us a prophetic word, even if the Bible were a guidebook that spelled out exactly what to do in any and every situation, God would still desire to speak to His children.

How do I know?

I have children.

I love to be with my children. I love to share my heart with them, to let them know how much I love and appreciate them, to encourage them, to comfort them.

Do we imagine that God thinks less of His own children?

Suppose I wrote a guidebook for my children, and every time they wanted to talk to me, I shook my head and said, "No. I won't talk to you. Read my book."

Understand that I'm not downplaying the importance of the Bible. I love spending time in God's Word, and I encourage you to do the same. But I am saying that God has a heart for His children, and He wants to share

---

[316] Even though I don't prophesy whom to marry, the Lord has given me words that have helped people with that decision, e.g., the golf story in Chapter 2.

that heart with them in many different ways.

As Christians we believe in a personal God who is concerned with every aspect of our lives. Why should it surprise us that God would want to speak in our lives on a one to one basis? Hosea prophesied, "In that day," declares the LORD, "you will call me, 'my husband;' you will no longer call me, 'my master.'[317] One of the greatest blessings in marriage is to be able to communicate with your spouse. Here Hosea prophesies there will be a time that we will no longer look at God as our Master, but we will look at Him as our husband. Husbands and wives spend a lot of time communicating. When we get a revelation that we are the bride of Christ, then we begin to understand God's desire to talk to us on a personal basis. I thank the Lord that He gave us the Bible as a primary source to get to know Him, but I also thank the Lord that He wants to also speak to us on a personal basis.

Jesus,[318] Peter,[319] John,[320] Jude[321] and Paul[322] all predicted that there would be false prophets in the last days. Jesus warned us to watch out for false prophets who would come to deceive. If all prophets are false now that the Bible is complete, then why didn't one of these men of God clear up the confusion by saying, "In the last days everyone who claims to be a prophet or attempts to prophesy is a false prophet, because you will have the written Word of God

---

[317] Hosea 2:16
[318] Matthew 24:11 etc.
[319] 2 Peter 2:1
[320] 1 John 4:1
[321] Jude 11 & context
[322] 1 Timothy 4:1+

and that is all you need."

The reason is simple: Not all prophets are false and not all prophecies are untrue. If there are false prophets, then there must be true prophets. Our job is to discern who is false and who is true.

Stop and think for a moment about the church. Consider how many problems and abuses there are. Churches split or some members won't speak to each other. Some pastors get involved in scandal and sin, and embarrass the cause of Christ.

God knows all of this. But the church is still the body of Christ here on this earth.

The same could be said about marriage. About families. About employment. About freedom.

Some oppose prophecy because they've seen it used the wrong way. And, yes, there are abuses. Yes, there are false prophets. But, as the previous chapters have demonstrated, the prophetic gift is still an instrument in God's hand for good.[323]

When I take an honest look at Scripture, I must conclude with Paul, "Follow the way of love and eagerly desire spiritual gifts, especially the gift of prophecy."[324]

So, then, what is prophecy?

Bill Hamon defines prophecy as, "God communicating His thoughts and intents to mankind."[325] The New Testament distinguishes prophecy[326] from

---

[323] 1 Corinthians 2:4-5 to cite just one example
[324] 1 Corinthians 14:1
[325] Bill Hamon, *Prophets and Personal Prophecy*, p. 29
[326] Greek: *propheteia* or *propheteuo*

preaching.[327]   Prophecy is to foretell or speak under Divine inspiration. Preaching is to announce good news. Thayer's lexicon elaborates:

> *Prophecy means to utter forth, declare a thing which can only be known by divine revelation; to break forth under sudden impulse in lofty discourse or in praise of divine counsels.*

One Old Testament word[328] for prophecy conjures up images of flowing, boiling up, bubbling up or over, gushing out, pouring forth words. Another Old Testament word[329] means to speak on behalf of another.

Simply put, prophecy is God speaking His word and His will to mankind.

Prophecy can be divided into two major categories: foretelling and forthtelling. God sometimes shares or *foretells* future plans or intents to a person, body of believers or a nation. Much of prophecy, however, is forthtelling. In other words, God declares through the prophet what he wants a person, body of believers or a nation to do or to understand. These are "now" words, not future words. God desires us to know right now what He is feeling toward us or what he wants us to do. Many of these prophetic words deal with our past hurts, pains, and decisions.

---

[327]   Greek: *euaggelizo*
[328]   Hebrew: *naba*
[329]   Hebrew: *nabbi*

Prophecy occurs at five levels:

Level # 1. The Bible is prophecy

Above all, you must understand that no prophecy of Scripture came about by the prophet's own interpretation.21 For prophecy never had its origin in the will of man, but men spoke from God as they were carried along by the Holy Spirit.[330]

From Genesis 1 to Revelation 22 the Scriptures bring forth God's will to our lives. Although prophecies may fail,[331] the Word of our God will abide forever.[332] The Scriptures instruct us to judge prophecies, but nowhere does it tell us to judge the written and inspired Word of God. The highest ranking of inspiration is the written Word of God.

Level # 2: The spirit of prophecy.

Sometimes the spirit of prophecy or prophetic song is so strong that those who are not prophets and those who do not have the gift of prophecy can prophesy. When the Spirit of God fell on Moses' elders everyone prophesied.[333] King Saul, even when he was totally backslidden, prophesied.[334] Caiphas prophesied even though he was

---

[330] 2 Peter 1:20-21
[331] 1 Corinthians 13:8
[332] Isaiah 40:8
[333] Numbers 11:25-29
[334] 1 Samuel 10:10-11, 18:10, 19:20-24

primarily responsible for putting Christ to death.[335] Sometimes the spirit of prophecy is so heavy that anyone can prophesy. Other times, a spirit of praise and worship invades a church and prophetic songs are stirred up.[336]

Level # 3: The gift of prophecy.

The gift of prophecy is spontaneously given to believers. Frequently mentioned in the New Testament,[337] the gift of prophecy is not given to a believer because of spiritual maturity, but is given to edify, comfort and strengthen the body of Christ. Paul said we all can prophesy;[338] the gift of prophecy is for any believer who has a desire to be used of God. The Old Testament prophet, Joel, predicted this gift and the outpouring of God's Spirit for all believers in the last days.[339]

Level # 4: The prophetic office.

The Bible establishes a prophetic office in the church.[340] The prophetic office is for mature saints who are called of God to flow on a consistent basis in the important area of prophecy. Some of the functions include: foretelling, confirmation of ministries, rebuke, counsel of God, correction, direction, guidance, judgment, purification, and revelation. The prophetic office constantly

---

335 John 11:51
336 See Psalm 33:3; 40:3; 96:1; 98:1; 144:9; 149:1; Isaiah 42:10; Revelation 5:9; 14:3; Ephesians 5:19; Colossians 3:16
337 Acts 2:17; 1 Corinthians 12:10; 4:1, 3, 4, 6, 22, 24, 31, 39; I Thessalonians 5:20; Romans 12:6
338 1 Corinthians 14:31
339 Joel 2:28-29
340 See Ephesians 2:20; 4:11; 1 Corinthians 12:28; Acts 13:1

and accurately operates in the word of knowledge, word of wisdom, miracles and discerning of spirits.

Some believers assume that just because they are used by God in an occasional gift of prophecy that they are a prophet. To clear up this confusion, here are some differences between the gift of prophecy and the prophetic office.

The office of a prophet is constant and consistent, whereas the gift of prophecy is spontaneous and seasonal. A prophet, functioning in this office, gives specific direction, some of which may be confrontational, while a person with the gift of prophecy gives words that are encouraging and apply to the general body of Christ. The prophet operates at a higher level of anointing and accuracy than the person who moves in the gift of prophecy. The office of a prophet imparts spiritual gifts to others.[341] The person who is a prophet is generally recognized by a body of believers, has had ministerial training and has a mature Christian life, whereas the gift of prophecy can operate in any believer no matter how long they have been a Christian or how committed they are to Christ. The gift of prophecy operates within the saints or a minister for the general strengthening, encouraging, and comforting of the Church.[342]

Level # 5: The prophetic presbytery

The prophetic presbytery[343] is a group of mature, godly, anointed believers who function together to share

---

[341] Romans 1:11; 1 Timothy 4:14
[342] 1 Corinthians 12:10; 14:3,4
[343] 1 Timothy 4:14; Hebrews 6:1-2; Acts 13:1-3

prophetic revelation and confirmation of those called into leadership. They are also used to ordain church leaders, and give direction to the church as a whole.

What's the difference between psychics and prophets?

Psychics do not glorify Jesus. Prophets do. The Bible says, "the testimony of Jesus is the spirit of prophecy."[344] Do the words and prayer and prophecies bring people closer to Jesus? Are people getting born-again? The Bible warns us that in the last days there would be many false prophets. The Bible predicts that the antichrist will do signs and wonders that would deceive the elect if it were possible. Psychics and prophets may have similar words and see similar visions, but the prophetic will draw people to Jesus.

"Freely you have received, freely give."[345] Psychics charge $5.00 per minute, but true prophets of God don't prophesy for personal gain, they prophesy because of the calling and command of God in their lives. Don't get me wrong, it takes money for full-time prophets to live, but our purpose is not money or notoriety, our purpose is to bring glory and honor to the Lord Jesus. True prophets are not in it for profit.

The prophet lives his life by the Word of God. Our goal and purpose is to get people to seek God for themselves just as the Bereans sought the Word of God to see if these things were true.[346] This is why true prophets must be men and women of the Word of God. I personally

---

[344] Revelation 19:10
[345] Matthew 10:8
[346] Acts 17:11

try to read three to five chapters a day to safeguard myself from lying and deceptive spirits. Remember, "Every Word of God is flawless; he is a shield to those who take refuge in him. Do not add to his words, or he will rebuke you and prove you a liar."[347] Those who take refuge in God and His word will be shielded. As Satan unleashes his deception in our age, we need the Word of God more than ever. We know that we prophesy in part[348] and know in part, but we also believe that the Word of God is 100% accurate. True prophets have the fear of God. They have no desire to add or subtract from the Word of God, lest they be judged by the true Judge.

True prophets know that every prophecy must be judged by other prophets according to what God has already spoken. Two or three prophets should speak, and the others should weigh carefully what is said.[349] Psychics are lone rangers and have little or no regard for the church.

How do you tell if someone is a false prophet? Or a true prophet who just made a mistake? How do you test prophecies?

Balaam gave true prophecies, but he was a false prophet.[350] Huldah was a true prophet, but her prophetic word did not come true.[351] So how can you tell the difference?

---

[347] Proverbs 30:5-6
[348] 1 Corinthians 13:9
[349] 1 Corinthians 14:29
[350] See Numbers 22-24, 31:16, 31:8, Joshua 13:22, Jude 11, Revelation 2:14
[351] 2 Chronicles 34:22-28 esp. v. 28 compared to 35:22-24

Jesus said, "by their fruit you will recognize them."[352] False prophets are people pleasers,[353] greedy for gain,[354] able to be bribed.[355] They tell people what they want to hear.[356] I call that the pathetic prophetic. They dabble in witchcraft[357] and divination.[358] They "dishearten the righteous with their lies,"[359] and prophesy from their own imagination.[360] They are ever popular with men,[361] but heartless toward God.

True prophets, on the other hand, are misjudged by the self-righteous crowd.[362] While true prophets are not infallible, the predictions of false prophets don't stand the test of time.[363]

When looking at a prophet, ask these kinds of questions: Is his or her life and ministry based on the Word of God? Does the ministry produce good fruit? Is he or she accountable and under authority? Does his or her lifestyle glorify God?[364]

I'm nauseated by "feel good" prophets who give words like, "You are going to be a millionaire," "You will

---

[352] Matthew 7:15-16
[353] See 1 Kings 22
[354] Jude 11
[355] Nehemiah 6:12
[356] Jeremiah 14:13
[357] Ezekiel 13:17-18
[358] Numbers 24:1
[359] Ezekiel 13:22
[360] Ezekiel 13:2
[361] Luke 6:26
[362] E.g., Luke 7:39
[363] Ezekiel 13, Jeremiah 28:9, 1 Samuel 9:6
[364] 1 Thessalonians 1:5; 5:12, Hebrews 13:7, 2 Timothy 3:10, Ephesians 6:21

have a world-wide ministry," or "You are an apostle." Obviously, there are Christians who make millions and help fund the gospel. There are Christians who have a world-wide ministry. But not every believer is going to fall into one of these categories. Most believers are never going to fall into one of these three categories. That doesn't mean that they are second-class or unspiritual. Many of the most caring and committed Christians have modest incomes, have a moderate influence on others and are called to a helps ministry. Yet, they are some of the most content, fun-loving, stress-free and shining examples of true Christians. Children and servants, according to Jesus, are the greatest in the kingdom of God.[365] It comes as no surprise, then, that most people in the body of Christ are average people who have an intimate love for Jesus. Even if these prophetic words of becoming a millionaire, an apostle or having a world-wide ministry are true, they are rarely fulfilled. Why? The bigger the ministry, the greater the commitment and the more intense the pruning. Most of us bail out when it gets too hot. The fact is the road to heavenly success is through failure, rejection, pain and perspiration. I wish I could say it was an overnight process, but it is not. It is a lifetime process. Those who are willing to pay the price will enjoy the prize.

Everyone makes mistakes. Prophets do too.[366] If you make a mistake in your prophesying, that doesn't make you a false prophet any more than a mistake in a teaching session makes you a false teacher. But, if you refuse to

---

[365] Matthew 18:1-4, Mark 9:35
[366] See Chapter 5

admit your mistakes, if you refuse to allow other prophets to judge your words, if you refuse to submit to authority, if you disregard the Word of God, then you are headed for serious trouble.

The Bible says, "Do not put out the Spirit's fire; do not treat prophecies with contempt. Test everything. Hold on to the good. Avoid every kind of evil."[367] Prophecies can be tested.

Here are some questions to ask when judging a word of prophecy: Does it line up with the Word of God?[368] Are other prophets in agreement with the word?[369] Does it stand the test of time?[370] Does it resonate with other mature Christians? Many times, I have a word for someone -- it makes no sense to that person -- but it does make sense to a pastor, a parent, or a family member. Remember that mistakes occur more often in the interpretation of the word than in the word itself.[371]

Why do some prophecies fail?

Prophecies fail for many reasons. They may fail because the prophet was mistaken or was lying.[372] They may fail because the party involved failed to meet stated or implied conditions.[373] They may seem to fail because

---

[367]   1 Thessalonians 5:19-22
[368]   Proverbs 30:5-6
[369]   1 Corinthians 14:29
[370]   Luke 2:51, Jeremiah 28:9
[371]   E.g., John 21:23
[372]   E.g., 1 Kings 22
[373]   This was probably the case in the prophecy of Huldah regarding the death of Josiah, 2 Chronicles 34:22-28 esp. v. 28 compared to

someone got the word right, but the interpretation wrong.[374] Remember the woman with the snake around her neck. She heard the word, but had no idea what it meant.[375]

Sometimes, because of sin and neglect, prophecies fail to come to pass. Consider this passage:

> *27 Now a man of God came to Eli and said to him, "This is what the Lord says: 'Did I not clearly reveal myself to your father's house when they were in Egypt under Pharaoh? 28 I chose your father out of all the tribes of Israel to be my priest, to go up to my altar, to burn incense, and to wear an ephod in my presence. I also gave your father's house all the offerings made with fire by the Israelites. 29 Why do you scorn my sacrifice and offering that I prescribed for my dwelling? Why do you honor your sons more than me by fattening yourselves on the choice parts of every offering made by my people Israel?' 30 "Therefore the Lord, the God of Israel, declares: 'I promised that your house and your father's house would minister before me forever.' But now the Lord declares: 'Far be it from me! Those who honor me I will honor, but those who despise me will be*

35:22-24
[374] E.g., John 21:23
[375] See Chapter 4

disdained.[376]

On the bright side, repentance can turn around a prophecy of judgment. Jonah predicted Nineveh's destruction. But when the people of Nineveh repented, God relented and withheld His hand of judgment.[377] Was Jonah a false prophet because Nineveh was not destroyed in forty days? Obviously not.

A final word

You are embarking on a wonderful adventure with God. Prophets and their work are dear to the heart of God. If you stay true to the Lord, His hand will be with you. He will get you past all the obstacles; He will take you by the hand and encourage you every step of the way.

I would love to hear about your journey. Drop me a line and let me know how it's going.

Tom Stamman
Impact Ministries International
PO Box 240135
Apple   Valley,   Minnesota   55124

---

[376] 1 Samuel 2:27-30
[377] Jonah 3:4, 10

Order additional copies of
The Blue-Collar Prophet:
How & Why God Wants to Speak Through You!

**Order on-line with a credit card:
visit http://www.creativeadvantage.us/books/**

Or order through the mail

Quantity _____ x $10 = $ _____
Add shipping & handling   +$4.00 _____

Total enclosed: $ _____
Ship to:
Name _____

Address_____

City State Zip _____

Mail your order to:
Impact Ministries International
PO Box 240135
Apple Valley, Minnesota 55124
Please include your phone number in case there are questions about your order.

2/18/04 Tom -